how to catch
and keep
a vampire

A STEP-BY-STEP GUIDE TO LOVING
THE BAD AND THE BEAUTIFUL

DIANA LAURENCE

SELLERS
PUBLISHING

contents

how to catch and keep
a vampire

This book is dedicated to David,
who doesn't need to be a vampire to be completely lovable.

The author is greatly indebted to Sellers Publishing and particularly Robin Haywood, for wanting to publish a handbook for vampirophiles, and discovering this writer whom they suspected had some knowledge on the subject. My special thanks to Conner, Colin, Gunnar, Mordred, Aidan, and Sven for their contributions, and the vampire community for their support.

www.howtocatchandkeepavampire.com

Published by Sellers Publishing, Inc.

Copyright © 2009 Sellers Publishing, Inc.

Text copyright © 2009 Diana Laurence

All rights reserved.

Edited by Robin Haywood

Sellers Publishing, Inc.
161 John Roberts Road, South Portland, Maine 04106
For ordering information:
(800) 625-3386 toll-free
(207) 772-6814 fax

Visit our Web site: www.sellerspublishing.com • E-mail: rsp@rsvp.com

ISBN 13: 978-1-4162-0552-4
Library of Congress Control Number: 2009928617

Disclaimer: This is a work of imagination in which you are invited to find as much reality as possible. All immortal characters appearing in this work are as real as vampires generally are. Any resemblance to real persons, living or dead, is purely coincidental, with a few exceptions (and you know who you are). Of course, all the *un*dead depicted herein are spot on, and called by their right names.

10 9 8 7 6 5 4 3 2 1

Printed and bound in the United States of America

• THE KEEPING •

introduction

So You Want to Date a Vampire

You tell me you want to date a vampire. My reply: Well, naturally!

And here all along you've been afraid to admit it, afraid it was weird and shocking and indicative of your need to see a therapist. Nonsense. In point of fact, nothing could be more natural or understandable.

I can guess what you're thinking now: "This author, this Diana — she doesn't realize I'm serious. She doesn't realize I'm talking about the real deal, not just some guy who dresses in black, wears sunglasses at night, and uses twinkly white body powder. I mean a real vampire, with the mind control, the biting, all that."

Yeah. Got it. I can't stand those posers either. As if clothes and haircut and looking out of the tops of your eyes were all it took.

I know exactly what you mean: a real vampire. With the questionable moral character, the hypnotic gaze, the paralyzing bite . . . all that great stuff. You've seen enough movies, read enough books, spent enough hours fantasizing about him pinning you to the wall with his stare and approaching you with that graceful gait, lips slightly parted, desperate hunger in his eyes. . . . And you've had enough of the fantasy already! Why can't you meet one, talk to one, maybe forge a bond, spark a genuine romance? Is that so much to ask?

Well, I'm here to tell you your longings for a bloodsucking companion are not in vain. And I will not be wasting your time with bad vampire puns like "in vein." You can meet a vampire, you can woo and win him, you can forge the kind of relationship you've dreamed of. You can catch and keep a vampire, because I'm going to tell you how.

And how do I know exactly? What are my credentials? Well, my credentials are Mordred, Conner, Aidan, Gunnar, and the other many and assorted vampires of my acquaintance. My credentials are years of vampire dating experience. And just as important, I really, truly understand why women like you and me (and men, too) are in love with vampires. I know why it's normal, and healthy, and exciting. I know its thrills and its dangers. I know how it can drag you down, but I also know how it can lift you up, even with that "undead" thing going on. I know how a vampire relationship can be achieved and conducted in harmony with your everyday existence. I also know a couple of vampires who actually love garlic shrimp.

And I know the secret of the red satin ribbon: both its benefits . . . and its risks.

So I'm going to share with you all my secrets and impart to you all my wisdom, and let these blood-drinking companions of mine teach you all they taught me. By the time we're done you'll know all you need to realize your dreams of bringing a real vampire into your life, and how to live to tell the romantic tale.

I'm not claiming this quest is without its challenges. Having a successful relationship never is. And it's even tougher when you throw in the special problems of being with a vampire: his ego, the crazy hours, your inability to deny him anything, his natural aversions to garlic and monogamy. There will be days that being in love with a vampire will seem like, for lack of a better word, a curse. But take heart; I'm here to be your guide, and show you that you do have the wherewithal to balance your vampirophilia with a full, happy, successful life. By the time we're done, you'll comprehend these unique, terrible, wonderful beings, and I hope you'll also better understand yourself.

Okay, so now you're shaking your head. You're waiting for the other shoe to drop. Surely sooner or later I'm going to get around to telling you that you've got to get over this vampire thing and content yourself with "reality." Friend, that's the last thing you'd ever hear from me! Anyone who'd say that has a funny view of reality. And you don't want to know what Mordred would do to anyone who said such a thing to his face . . . he can perform some amazing moves with those fingernails of his.

So trust me: I respect you and sympathize with you in the best and worst way. If you think for a minute I'm going to end this little dissertation with some "well, it's been fun, now back to your regularly scheduled life," you are dead wrong. Or undead wrong.

Okay, there may be an occasional pun.

Enough intro; let's get started. And we'll start where you obviously need to begin: with a look at exactly why any sane person is dying to catch and keep a vampire.

chapter 1

What's a Vampire Got That My Boyfriend Hasn't Got?

if you're like most vampirophiles, there have been times when you've questioned yourself. Like you just watched Tom Cruise, Stephen Moyer, or Robert Pattison doing a wonderful portrayal of a vampire, and enjoyed the actor's fine representation of the blood-drinking act. You see him, his chin smeared with blood . . . and you're in a paroxysm of desire.

"What about this scene is sexy?" you ask yourself. "Am I out of my mind?"

On its face, the bloodsucking concept is not appealing, I'll admit. Certainly no one willingly invites leeches or mosquitoes into her boudoir. But there are many other elements to the vampire mystique, and taken all together, they have an appeal that mortals find irresistible.

So let's talk about why blood-drinking beings are so attractive. To do that, we need to more fully understand what makes a vampire, particularly modern vampires.

NIGHT AND DAY, HE IS THE ONE

In case you weren't aware, vampire society has evolved over the centuries just like mortal society has. While we've gone through periods of progress like the Renaissance, the Industrial Revolution, and the Technology Age, vampires have been conducting progress of their own. Can I give you an example? Yes, in two words . . . "Liquid Shade." Liquid Shade is an elixir today's immortals drink to ward off the damaging effects of the sun's rays. Yes, thanks to advancements in vampire labs ("Better unliving through chemistry"), now the undead can move among us during the day. They can hold down jobs (because Liquid Shade isn't cheap), take cruises to the tropics, go to early-bird sales at the mall, and do pretty much everything except get a tan.

In spite of the advantages of daylight living, most vampires remain nocturnal, and here's why: one of the key elements of vampire cachet is their after-dark mystique. Here's the first item to put on your "vampires trump my boyfriend" list: they are Creatures of the Night. For some, it's just for marketing purposes; for others, it's truly because darkness suits their nefarious lifestyle. But either way, it's sexy. Nighttime lends vampires the air of mystery, the sinister vibe that is so alluring. They come to pick you up on horseback or on a Harley at night, they gaze at you over a candlelit dinner at night, they creep into your room at night.

Your boyfriend invariably is forced to interact with you during normal daylight hours. That is, he has to get up in the morning for class or his job. You may have met him at a club under low lights, but he will be hard pressed to date you more than a few times and not let you see him in daylight . . . or worse yet, the unflattering glare of a K-Mart's florescents or something. Your boyfriend must occasionally go to a K-Mart — toothpaste doesn't deliver itself — but a vampire, believe me, wouldn't be caught dead in a K-Mart and has other ways of obtaining toothpaste.

Which leads us to another great advantage of the vampire: his hypnotic power.

RESISTANCE IS FUTILE

Hypnotists . . . now there's another example of the interesting types of men we ladies are into. Guys who can mesmerize are a popular romantic archetype in their own right, that's for sure. You know the kind of thing I mean: like when the evil hypnotist gets the heroine in his clutches by using that "look deep into my eyes" line. Then things get all deliciously swirly and the next thing you know, she's putty in his hands.

By the way, your mortal boyfriend would never have the chutzpah to use that line on you; he'd be too embarrassed. Vampires do not get embarrassed. They do whatever works, and that is why at least six vampires have used the "look deep into my eyes" line on me. And I totally loved it every time.

So, vampires are the real deal when it comes to hypnotism. If one of them gives you the eye and turns on the power, it's useless to resist. Well, not completely useless: When you're with a trustworthy vampire (and I'll give you tips for determining "trustworthy" in the next chapter),

I've found it's often fun to try to resist for awhile and then surrender hopelessly. The really talented vampires have mastered their power so that they can make you feel like you're losing your will to them, but they give you enough wiggle room so you can struggle awhile before capitulating. In fact, a good way to tell a new vampire from an old one is how well he can control his hypnotic skills. A newbie will take complete hold in a flash and miss out on all that delightful tussling.

PERFECT BEINGS BEING PERFECT

Okay, so I just touched upon another key vampire trait that we need to address further: his self-confidence. This is where a blood-drinking guy really has it all over your boyfriend. Regular males have the definite disadvantage of being resistible. I don't care how hot your boyfriend is, there are still times, like when he has the flu or won't stop talking about woodworking, when he is eminently resistible. Vampires don't get the flu, obviously. And although some of them like woodworking, they can tell if a woman doesn't, so if they feel like discussing bandsaws, planers and routers, they will hypnotize you into being completely into the subject first.

Meanwhile, regular guys lack self-confidence because they are subject to natural laws like gravity and mortality. When you know that you can't crawl up a building, or survive a gunshot wound to the heart, or be sure a girl will want to go to a movie with you, it's tough. You can't expect mortal guys to have the charming cockiness of vampires, who know they can run two-minute miles and win "American Idol" any day of the week.

Yes, vampiric perfection plays a big part here, too. You know why only great-looking and sexy guys are cast as vampires in movies and TV shows? Because all vampires are great-looking and sexy. I don't care if they looked like Ronald McDonald before they were turned; after the undead thing takes hold, they will be Chippendale material. Wait, let me amend that, because not all women (myself included) are attracted to that kind of stilted, forced "hotness." A vampire always has a handsomeness about him that is more than skin deep, more than good cheekbones and perfect hair. He possesses this essential confidence that resonates throughout his entire being: eyes, smile, voice, carriage, heart, and soul. It's not just mind-jolting good looks: it's poise, wit, competence, and talent.

Are you still questioning why you are attracted to vampires? But wait, there's more.

ALL HE NEEDS IS BLOOD

Ironically, another common asset among the immortal is vulnerability. Because nothing a guy can do hooks a girl more effectively than the suggestion that he needs her. If I had a dollar for every vampire who's said to me, "I'm immortal, but I can't live without you," I could treat us both to lobster dinners. We women are such suckers for guys we think we can help. Problem is, being perfect and immortal and all, vampires very rarely need us. I'm not saying there aren't rare cases when a needy vampire meets a mortal woman who fulfills him . . . there are just not that many needy vampires. Well, other than needing blood, but they can get that easily enough.

Another one of the great advancements of modern vampires concerns their diet. As mortal science has proven with the development of synthetic insulin, our vampire friends long ago developed synthetic human blood. Why is our science so far behind their's in this department? Well, as you might guess, it was something of a priority in vampire society. While we've been busy with things like penicillin and vaccines and cloning sheep, immortals didn't have such a variety of concerns. They pretty much need blood, period.

So if some vampire feeds you the line, "I haven't fed in three days . . . without your blood I'll perish," take it from me: he is full of it. And full of blood, too. It's not even particularly expensive — nothing like Liquid Shade.

That said, vampires still really get off on feeding. There are a couple of reasons for this. For one thing, as Gunnar put it to me once, "synthblood is like skim milk; human blood is like a chocolate shake." Real blood is tastier, more effective, an all-around better time. Additionally, as Colin once described it, "Drinking synthblood is like riding a bike, drinking human blood is like driving a Ferrari." Vampires enjoy the *act* of drinking blood as much as the blood itself, for much the same reason as we "victims" do.

. . . *follow me to page 18*

an alternative beverage choice

Speaking of synthblood, *you* should invest in
a small supply. I'll let my friend Megan explain
from personal experience just why.

I admit I'm the kind of vampirophile who likes to flirt, literally, with danger. After all, vampires pretty much equal danger . . . it's their most endearing trait, if you ask me. So when I spot an immortal across the room and he's giving me a come-hither look, I'm sure not going to respond by going-thither instead.

The undead bring out the crazy fool in me, but I'm not a total crazy fool. I figured out a pretty good tip I would like to share with other vampire lovers: I keep a nice supply of synthblood at my house. I've done it for a long time, as a precaution, but on one occasion it came in really handy.

I met Paolo in a grocery store, hunting for oregano in the spice section, when we started talking about lasagne recipes. He volunteered to make me dinner. I could tell by the look in his eyes that he was not so much interested in proving his skills with a chef's knife as his skills with his teeth. He appeared fierce enough to make most women nervous. The thing is, I really dig fierce.

Paolo's lasagne was superb. His bite was even better. Fortunately, I have enough experience with vampires that I kept my head rather than blissing out into oblivion. Unfortunately, Paolo was one of those immortals who lose track of the volume of consumption. He drank past the pint level till I was feeling very swoony, and not in a good way. My "please stop" was enough to make him pause, but I could tell by the urgency of his feeding that Paolo was ravenous.

I quickly broke out a bag of synthblood, warmed it in a mug in the microwave, and thereby had a decent alternative to offer him besides my lifeblood. Paolo wasn't a bad guy, just really hungry, so he accepted gracefully.

So take a tip from me: a famished vampire can be a handful. It's wise to have a couple of options available for satisfying that hunger, one of which is not you. XO Megan

SEDUCTION STILL PLAYS IN THE 21ST CENTURY

Let's talk about the inherent allure of "donating blood" to a vampire. While I'm sure Bram Stoker intended to horrify his male readers and make his female readers faint, he failed to appreciate certain things about women. Even in these post-women's-lib days, the majority of females are hardwired to enjoy the occasional bout of surrender. We can and should allow for perfectly natural deviations (it takes all kinds to make a world), but the basic essence of courtship remains constant: The male seduces, the female is seduced.

In today's world, where women have achieved desirable equality with men in most ways, a lot of women find something missing from their day-to-day existence. While they drive themselves to meet their boyfriends at restaurants, go dutch to the movies, omit "obey" from their wedding vows, etc., today's liberated and independent women are looking for ways to indulge that largely anachronistic urge to yield to a stronger being.

Now, your mortal boyfriend is certainly not going to consider grabbing you by the shoulders, pressing you into a wall, and demanding you yield something precious, like your lifeblood, to him. Heck, nowadays he's afraid to open a door for you!

A vampire, on the other hand, doesn't give a rat's tush what is politically correct or socially acceptable. He sees you, at best, as someone he wants desperately, and at worst, as prey. He is the very essence of male aggression and domination. A nice vampire tries to keep those traits in obeisance to politeness and decency; a bad vampire indulges them. If that terrifies you, so much the better.

Okay, let's pause a minute here. I want you to go back and reread that paragraph. After you have, ask yourself honestly: Did you get the little electric thrill when you read "A nice vampire tries to keep those traits in obeisance to politeness and decency"? Or was it when you read "a bad vampire indulges them. If that terrifies you, so much the better"?

Ay, there's the rub. The final, and most paradoxical, reason why a vampire is better than your boyfriend is that he's worse. You honestly don't want your boyfriend to be cruel, or vicious, or wildly self-indulgent. Your vampire, on the other hand, is a completely different story. We'll go into this phenomenon more in the next couple of chapters, but for now, suffice it to say, I think you know what I mean.

IMMORTALS WIN — AND YOU'RE ACQUITTED

Well, your honor, I rest my case. Your boyfriend or significant other could be good-looking, smart, funny, capable, and really nice, and still pale by comparison to your literally pale vampire. My point here is not to dis your boyfriend; I'm certainly not suggesting you break up with him in order to dedicate yourself to vampire love. No, what I'm trying to prove to you is that there's nothing weird or wrong about your yearning to be with a blood-drinking guy. Seriously, you'd have to be crazy not to feel that way.

I am a firm believer in this: Every woman is entitled to pursue, embrace, and indulge her vampirophilia as a natural part of her feminine makeup. Besides, shame is always useless when you're dealing with vampires. They either laugh it off with one of those low, sexy chuckles of theirs, or they prey on it ("See how you desire me so much that you do not hesitate to commit this dreadful act," etc.).

No shame allowed, my friends . . . however, I do advise *caution*. We can't forget that while vampires are beautiful, sexy, and endlessly amusing, they can also be deadly dangerous. And, unfortunately, there are some among us vampirophiles who find themselves strangely drawn to the most dangerous, unpredictable, treacherous immortals. Yes, I admit it: that would be me. Why do we desire the very vampires who threaten us most? Well, I'll try to explain that, too. Because before you start your vampire catching, I want you to be better prepared than I was.

But enough of the scary stuff. There are plenty of kind, amiable vampires out there, so let's begin by getting to know one of them. . . .

Ethan was my first real vampire. I met him in a shopping mall food court.

This particular food court had a grand piano in the center. I was alone at one of the sticky little tables with a medium diet cola, resting my feet and quenching my thirst. This shiny black piano was just sitting there, maybe fifteen feet away. There was a placard in the little metal sign standing next to it that read, "2:00-3:00 / Ethan DeMille, Pianist / Baldwin Piano Courtesy of Hellman's Pianos."

I checked my watch; it was just two o'clock. And then, with the utmost punctuality, the performer appeared. From where I didn't quite notice. But suddenly there he was, dressed in a charcoal gray oxford shirt with the cuffs turned up, and black jeans. He sat down at the piano and began to play.

And such music! It is never easy to do justice to music in words, and, in this case, the cause is hopeless. For it was supernatural music: music that carried upon its sound actual, literal emotion. Passion and vitality, joy and desire wafted through the air, from the sounding board to my ears . . . from his fingers to my soul.

I sat, staring, my hand clutching my waxed cup. This man couldn't possibly be as beautiful as he seemed. Looking at him, I found myself realizing I had never seen a perfect man before, not even in a magazine ad or in a movie, because no one looked like him. He had a face that conveyed both the clean freshness of youth and the intriguing charm of experience. His eyes were aquamarine blue, his hair black and sleek and slightly long. His bangs veiled his eyes when he looked down at the keyboard. I could tell from the way he played that he didn't need to look at the keys. He did it because he knew the veiling of his eyes was so becoming.

I liked that about him. I liked that he had such a fine-tuned sense of what to do to be alluring, and no inclination whatsoever to do otherwise. Clearly, he wanted to draw me in, to capture me, and every gesture, every note, strove toward that goal. How can I describe the joy of being wanted that much? Until then I had only experienced such a feeling occasionally in dreams. But why me? Why had he chosen me to charm with his look and his sublime piano playing?

Interestingly, when I managed through sheer force of will to look around me, I found that no one else in the food court was paying particular attention to him. I saw a few people moving slightly to the music, so I knew everyone could hear just fine, but I found no one else reacting as I was, with awe and desperate yearning.

Later on, Ethan would explain to me that, in fact, the hard part of this little performance was not attracting me, but preventing the few hundred other people within earshot from taking particular note of him. Vampires are, after all, inherently attractive. Most of the time they prefer to go unnoticed. I didn't know it at the time, but one of the first things a vampire must practice is making himself appear ordinary to those around him.

For me, he simply didn't conceal his true self.

I knew he was a vampire. After all, I'd read about vampires, and, more significantly, written about them, and the sense of recognition was immediate. If Ethan had the charisma of, say, a rock star, I would have recognized that for what it was: the larger-than-life charm of someone who makes his living on the stage, exuding sex appeal and bravado. Ethan's charisma made a rock star seem like one of those morons in the old "Mr. Microphone" commercials. It was so-rich-you-can-taste-it charisma, sir-may-I-please-have-another-helping charisma.

As for the "why me?" question, I asked him that later. He said it was simply because vampires like people who like vampires, and he could tell I did. I didn't really find that an adequate response, but I let it go because at the time it didn't matter to me as much as, well, letting him bite me.

But back to me, and Ethan, and the piano, and the food court. I sat there in my plastic chair, saying to myself, *"This guy is a vampire, why else would I feel this way?"* I watched the way his hands lifted and fell on the keys, the exquisite grace of each individual finger, and ached to kiss them. I saw the light catch in his black hair, and the unalterable darkness in his blue eyes behind the veil of his bangs. I saw his pale, pearlescent cheeks and wondered if they would be cool to the touch. He's a *vampire*, I thought, and wondered how I would bear it if I didn't end up swooning in his embrace.

But I needn't have worried about that. His music had me, he had me, and the rapture was all mine.

FAQS ABOUT THE UNDEAD

Q: Can vampires fly?

A: Vampires have taken me flying, but I still suspect they can't actually fly. You see, vampires are very aware of the mortal fascination with flying and the romantic connotations of same. That would give them reason enough to simply hypnotize people into believing they are being taken airborne. But if vampires were truly swooping around, wouldn't the FAA have taken note by now? And for people like me who are prone to motion sickness, this is actually a boon. A vampire will look deeply into your eyes and say, "Now we will fly, and you won't get airsick." Works wonderfully well, and, to my mind, renders the issue of their actual flying abilities moot.

Q: Do modern vampires sleep in coffins?

A: Believe it or not, vampires of yore clung to superstitions just like mortals of yore did. One of those was the idea that in order to stay immortal, you had to sleep either on the soil of your origins, or in a box with some of it. This wasn't as much of an issue when your alternative was a straw mattress and scratchy woolen blankets. But with the advent of the feather-bed, vampires began to relinquish the practice, and by the time the Sleep Number Bed was developed, the whole coffin thing was completely passé.

Q: Can vampires turn into bats or other creatures?

A: A couple of my immortal friends have told me there was a time when they could, but both those guys love to b.s. about vampires' fabulous feats. (Obviously, they neglected to hypnotize me into believing them.) At any rate, modern vampires don't transmogrify. When you're that great-looking, why would you want to look like anything else? In a similar vein, though, vampires can hypnotize and control animals. When they do it with dogs it's no big deal — dogs are inherently all about obedience. But with cats it's pretty spectacular — try getting a cat to do what you want without the benefit of mind control.

chapter 2

Is It Possible to Tame a Vampire?

on occasion I've found myself in a conversation with someone who is curious about vampire dating, and he or she will ask me, "Oh, but is it really possible to tame a vampire?"

When I hear that, I can't help but reply, "'Tame a vampire'? You don't *really* want to date a vampire, do you?"

When I speak of "catching" a vampire, I mean locating one and attracting his interest. When I speak of "keeping" a vampire, I'm talking about establishing a relationship with him. Neither one of these has anything to do with *taming*, as most people who want to date a vampire completely understand. Let me elaborate.

YOU COULDN'T IF YOU WANTED TO

You cannot tame a vampire, or, at least, you don't really want to for a number of reasons. First of all, one of the changes that occur with conversion is the acquisition of a predatory nature. It's just part of the package, along with the total loss of melanin in the skin and the pointy incisors. A vampire just can't help being wild and aggressive, at least under certain circumstances.

Besides that . . . just consider for a moment what "taming" is. It's a program that combines intimidation with reassurance, during which the tamer both proves himself trustworthy to the tamee, and establishes himself as the stronger party. Well, good luck convincing a creature that can break glass with a look that you are the stronger party. Meanwhile, vampires are in the enviable position of never having to be concerned about the trustworthiness of an opponent or victim. Immortality will do that for you: the being who is nearly impossible to hurt or kill generally has the upper hand.

. . . *follow me to page 30*

taming a vampire: a cautionary tale

My friend Beth will offer a very rare example of
the taming of a vampire. Her family secret will
illustrate the unfortunate result.

*My great-grandmother Patrice was born in the Vosges
Mountains in eastern France. Vampires loved that area of
Europe for its beautiful women and its superb wine. Patrice
was in love a with vampire named Christophe, and the two had
a remarkable relationship. But my great-grandmother had an
understandably desperate fear of aging, and constantly pictured
herself old, weak, and wrinkled while Christophe remained able
to attract his pick of the lovely girls of the district. She pleaded
with Christophe to make her immortal, but he refused.*

*Patrice thought her only alternative was to somehow tame
her vampire lover so he wouldn't stray. She'd heard stories that
a certain kind of silver found in the Vosges Mountains rendered
vampires docile and controllable, so she purchased some from
an old miner, and had it made into a chain with a lock. One
night, while Christophe slept, she locked the chain around his
ankle and threw the key into the river.*

*The silver worked its magic all right. Christophe gave up the
various charming vampire pursuits that had won Patrice's heart
in the first place. No more wild cavorting in the night, no more
triple-forte singing of romantic arias to express his adoration.
Instead, Christophe took up knitting and joined a book club.*

*He still drank my great-grandmother's blood on occasion,
but insisted on washing his hands first and using a napkin.*

*Patrice at seventy was indeed somewhat weak and wrinkled.
But she still had a hell of a lot more spunk and fire than her
handsome, youthful vampire consort. She carried her regret with
her to her grave.*

Ergo, there is pretty much no reason for a vampire to allow himself to be tamed. Obviously, you can't intimidate him into it. Likewise, there is no kind of psychological trickery you can use. Even the stupidest vampire will outmaneuver you in the end: as soon as it dawns on him that you're trying to dissuade him from his dominant, undomesticated ways, he'll put the kibosh on you right quick. And when I say "kibosh," I mean the swirly, immobilizing eyes followed by the chomp on the jugular.

SURE, TAME HIM . . . BWAHAHA!

Over the years I have confirmed this belief of mine by discussing this issue directly with a great many vampires. To a man (and including some females, too), they respond to the question, "Is it possible for you to be tamed?" with . . . wait for it . . . laughter.

Various kinds of laughter. I've gotten sarcastic sniggers, explosive guffaws, and low, menacing chuckles. Actually, sometimes it's fun to ask a vampire this, just because it may earn you one of those low, menacing chuckles. They are really kind of a turn-on, especially when accompanied by the lifting of one eyebrow and the line, "All right, let's go to your house and you can try to tame me."

Okay, now go back and reread that last. Gave you shivers, didn't it? Which leads me to my other point: Why would you *want* to tame a vampire?

We're starting to see a pattern here. When vampires are unpredictable, dangerous, arrogant, and threatening, we rather like it. All right, we *really* like it, even though that's counterintuitive. After all, when you're looking for a mortal mate, a boyfriend, or husband, these are not qualities on your must-have list. You're looking for a guy who is reliable, trustworthy, sensitive, kindhearted, willing to compromise and cooperate. You want a guy who is, in effect, tame. If you ask him to pick you up at 8 o'clock, you'd like to open your door at 8 o'clock and find him in your driveway. If you ask him to talk about something other than NASCAR, you'd like him to be willing to discuss classic alternative music.

On the other hand, when it comes to vampires, it's a whole other story. Take, for example, when you are digging in the trunk of your car, pulling out the last grocery bag, and you close the trunk and find your vampire suddenly standing there, leaning against the passenger door and grinning fiendishly. Why is his startling and rather unnerving appearance so exciting?

Or maybe you're looking at a long night of tax preparation or office work, and the doorbell rings. You have no time to entertain vampires tonight . . . you have a project due in the morning, and here he is on your porch asking to be let in. "No, Graham," you say, "I'm really sorry, but I just can't invite you in tonight." To which he responds, "Ah, but I think you can. I'm quite sure, in fact, that you really want to."

So who's taming whom? In point of fact, vampires are at the tippy-top of the "taming chain." Nobody tames like these guys. So I ask you, what could be a more absurd idea than you taming a vampire?

DON'T TRY THIS WITH YOUR BOYFRIEND

As I just demonstrated, the stuff vampires pull off just doesn't play as well when humans do it. I don't know if it's just the mind control talking or what, but it's amazing what vampires can do and come off as really attractive. Let a mortal man attempt these "taming" behaviors, and all you see before you is a stubborn, irascible, cranky guy — ironically, not good dating material at all. When I was younger, I tried dating a few men who were doing their best to emulate vampire behavior — pushiness, arrogance, self-absorption — only to find that they were basically just creeps. Funny how that works.

But when you're dealing with vampires, it's a totally different story. You don't mind the arrogance because, after all, it's totally justified. A man whose eyes sometimes appear to contain the known universe has a right to be cocky. And while vampires can be fierce and unpredictable, they usually temper that with impeccable manners. ("My darling, I hope you will do me the great honor of allowing me to pierce your glorious flesh with these unworthy teeth," etc.) Even the self-absorption, which is normally one of my least favorite traits, can have a certain charm. Sure, you sort of wish he'd ask how your day was, but it's generally more interesting talking about him: his experiences in Paris during the Renaissance, the time he subdued the Broadway star and took over the lead role in *Phantom of the Opera* for the night, and so on.

Case Study 102:

*Me, Gunnar, and how my attempts
to tame him backfired horribly.*

I met Gunnar in an all-night laundromat called Sudden Suds. I was waiting for my last load to dry; he was folding towels with incredible speed and precision.

Gunnar was obviously of Scandinavian origin, having hair and eyes that actually made his vampirically fair complexion seem totally natural. His hair was wavy and thick and appeared to be literally spun of gold; it gleamed so richly, even in the brash fluorescents of Sudden Suds. We seemed to be under the shimmering lighting of a jewelry store. His eyes were of the palest blue, and looking into them made me feel cold, but in a good way.

When I met Gunnar, the only vampire with whom I had experience was Ethan. I had no means of comparison to tell me that Ethan was quite a gentle, sweet-natured immortal. He persuaded me to do things quite subtly, never employing a lot of *sturm und drang*. I was frightened of Ethan because he was undead and could have at any time made me likewise. But Ethan himself never did anything deliberately to frighten me. Based on my knowledge of him, I had certain expectations of Gunnar.

One ought never to have certain expectations of a vampire.

As my clothes did circles in the dryer, I took furtive glances at Gunnar. I couldn't take my eyes off him. Every motion he made was like ballet; the way his hands smoothed over the towels made me ache deliciously. Our eyes met. He smiled in that way vampires often do: just slightly, but so potently you rejoice all the way to your toes at having been deemed worthy of the gesture.

I turned away with effort, and unloaded my clothes into the basket. I was just finishing when I felt a slight, cool breeze at my side. A silky voice murmured in my ear, "Let me fold those for you." Of course, I let him. How could I deny a vampire who does his own laundry?

As he worked his folding magic on my laundry, Gunnar invited me to have coffee (for my sake, I hoped it was someplace with better lighting). Over lattes at the coffee bar up the block, we chatted about his past, particularly a conversation he'd had once with Hans Christian Anderson about unrequited love and *The Little Mermaid*. My first impression was that Gunnar spoke in poetry. It worked as conversation, but it also struck me as poetry, rich in imagery, with the words carefully chosen for their aural effect.

When I drained my last sip of coffee, Gunnar said, "Take me home with you."

I had, by this time, already been thinking about the possibility of that, but the tone of his voice rather frightened me. It implied he was not merely making a suggestion. Feeling anxious, I replied, "Oh Gunnar . . . you seem really nice, but maybe we should get to know each other a little better first."

He reached across the table and took ahold of my wrist. His grip was very interesting: it caused me no pain, but I was absolutely convinced he could snap my bones effortlessly if he wanted to. I was scared. And then he said, "It amuses me that you believe you have an option."

Had he been just a mortal man, I would have called for aid and definitely deleted his number from my phone at my earliest opportunity. But, as you know by now, vampires are another story.

I told him quietly, "I really don't think it's a good idea. You see, when I was with Ethan, he was quite nice about never insisting."

"Oh, I'm not insisting," said Gunnar, his grip tightening and his lips forming a pleasant smile. "The way this works is, I get what I want, and you're totally, wonderfully happy about that."

All at once I realized my misstep. Gunnar was one of those vampires who always rise to a challenge. I think if I had gone along with his coming home with me when he first proposed it, we might have simply stayed up late watching *American Psycho* and then parted as new friends. But my insistence on exerting my will provoked him to prove himself the stronger.

Now don't picture Gunnar as some huge, menacing bully. He is really rather slight of build, and sweet of face, with a refined way of speaking and an airy tenor voice. He did not rise up as if to strike me. On the contrary, he lowered his chin in deference, and raised my hand to his lips as if to kiss it.

And then he dug his teeth into my wrist.

That was what he wanted, and as he so wisely predicted, after about ten seconds I was totally, wonderfully happy about it.

To his credit, Gunnar didn't drink long. After a minute or two he stopped, kissed my wrist, and wiped it and his mouth clean with his napkin. Then he raised his ice blue eyes to me and imparted a message I have never forgotten: "Diana," he said, "please remember, vampires are at the top of the taming chain."

Lesson learned.

UNTAMED AND EVIL TO BOOT

In fact, for people like me, the idea of a genuinely malicious vampire even has its appeal. I don't mean one of the decent types who just behave badly to amuse you; I mean the truly evil sort. Like Dr. Grey. Okay, now you know his name.

Dr. Steven Grey will be your model for the kind of vampire who can draw a girl in, just by his very nature and without use of supernatural trickery. I'm sure you've daydreamed about this sort. He scares you . . . deliciously. You can't trust him . . . and you love it. He is every inch a terrifying predator . . . and in your heart of hearts you wish to be his prey.

Dr. Grey, you will learn, is a member of the local immortal community who exemplifies the downside (think way down, as in hellish) of the vampiric nature. Most of the undead of my acquaintance shun him and warn their mortal friends to do likewise. Heaven knows, I got enough warning, and yet — why on earth would I want to risk associating with such a being? I guess I'm just an Extreme Mina, meaning Mina, the character from *Dracula* who ends up in his seductive clutches. Everyone has a little Mina in them, which is perfectly fine, but I have just a little too much Mina. Let me tell you what I mean.

LETTING MINA OUT

Now, a puzzle. What do these three things have in common?

- Teenagers fainting at the sight of the rock stars they idolize.
- Women trying to persuade their boyfriends to dress as pirates for Halloween.
- The insanely vast and ever-mounting number of times you have enjoyed your favorite vampire books and movies.

There is in most women a craving to release what I call our Inner Mina. The Inner Mina is that unswervingly Victorian element of your personality who would gladly turn the clock back a hundred years, give up the vote, wear a corset, and be subject to the vapors.

Please understand that I am a very independent woman. I don't enjoy wearing a bra, much less a corset. I'm not suggesting that vampirophiles like you and I are throwbacks to a bygone era. Nevertheless, I maintain that in the dark corners of our secret souls, where spooky violin music plays and there is sometimes a voiceover performed by Vincent Price, we women harbor an Inner Mina.

At every age, we read vampire books and watch vampire movies over and over so we can imagine ourselves as Mina, melting into Dracula's arms. We never tire of this fantasy of utter capitulation to the dangerous but imminently seductive power of the vampire. He is so dark, so foreboding . . . and yet promises such transcendent delights. All he asks is that you lose your will to him, and in return you will feel the glorious bliss of his domination. . . .

How delightful to be able to surrender to the vampire! Did I just forget decades of progress achieved by the women's movement? I couldn't help it, the vampire hit me with his swirly eyes and knocked it all right out of my head!

FINDING STRENGTH IN THE SWOON

And there's the key to the whole phenomenon: When you go all submissive and swoony in the presence of a vampire, it's really not your fault. You don't need to compromise your values or sacrifice your self-esteem; you didn't stand a chance against this immensely powerful immortal being and his dangerous mystical mind control. This is a good thing, a very good thing. Because I'm not here to recommend that you compromise your values: I'm a big fan of integrity. I don't want you to sacrifice your self-esteem: you should encourage it, defend it, and never do anything that demeans you.

Don't settle for ill treatment from anyone. Don't enable others who are trying to take advantage of you. These are not occasions when you ought to indulge your Inner Mina and turn into a Milquetoast.

The best, safest, most rewarding place to let Mina do her thing is when you're with one of the honorable vampires. For even though no vampire is tame, the good ones do play fair. Their rules are very simple: Let them feed on you when they want to, and let them get their way. They have no interest in demeaning or insulting you, disappointing you, making you look bad to friends, or cheating on you. (Well, regarding that last one: they will never cheat on the sly — they believe in full disclosure when it comes to infidelity. But more on that later.)

Over the years I've found an approach that works really well for me, and I think it might work for you, too. You can enjoy the delicious surrender, the utter helplessness your Inner Mina craves when you are in the company of your vampire. You can set aside considerations of practicality, social correctness, even prudency, and not worry about a thing. There's no point in trying to make a wise choice when you are sitting next to a guy who can dissolve your will by raising one perfect eyebrow.

Then when you are back in the everyday world, dealing with lunatic supervisors, gossiping friends, or even boyfriends who are proving to be genuine users, you may be surprised to find you have a spine of iron.

I have a personal pithy adage that sums up this principle nicely: "She who swoons for the swirly eyes trembles for no man, nor woman neither, so ha!" It is a pithy adage that has served me well and long.

DETERMINING WHEN IT'S NOT SO SAFE

As I said, decent vampires will not take advantage of your Mina. Evil ones, however, will. Can you tell them apart? Was I completely duped by this Dr. Grey person, blindsided and victimized without warning? (And I *will* get around to the details of that . . . I just need to work up to the horrifying and mortifying confessions a bit.)

To be perfectly honest, in fact you really *can* tell them apart. Trustworthy vampires only play at being bad, so that we mortals can indulge our Inner Mina. On the other hand, evil vampires are quite sincere in their badness — they don't do it for you, they do it for themselves. It's really not hard to tell the difference.

The difficulty comes in when you know the difference and, in some warped way, don't care. Even that I can sort of explain, and will, in the next chapter.

Nevertheless, if you pay a little attention and keep your wits about you, you truly can recognize the kind of vampire you want to avoid. If he's obsessed with undead superiority, determined to subjugate all living things, and gets off on convincing mortals to make dreadful, irreversible mistakes, do not sign up for his adult education class like I did. There are plenty of nice vampires around to provide you a safe environment where you can indulge yourself without fear, and reap the excellent benefits thereof.

FAQS ABOUT THE UNDEAD

Q: Is there a difference when a vampire bites you on the wrist, as opposed to the neck? What about other spots?

A: In terms of the significance of bite locations, you can pretty much apply your normal sense of the relative casualness vs. intimacy. Just as a kiss on the hand is more formal, cordial, or friendly than a kiss on the neck, etc., similar principles apply with vampire bites. Well-mannered vampires seldom "go right for the jugular." That said, you'd be amazed at the thrills some of them can achieve by a simple bite on the wrist. It's not like a handshake, I'll tell you that.

Q: Is it true that a vampire can only enter your house if you invite him?

A: Vampires really like to perpetuate this idea, but I'm convinced it's only a social convention. It's like this: I've never had a vampire ask to come into my house and not let him. I don't know anyone who has. But they make a big deal about the custom, and I believe it's simply to flaunt the fact that they always get an invitation. As if we didn't have enough reasons already to acknowledge their power over us, geez.

Q: Can all vampires lift one eyebrow?

A: I did bring that up more than once, didn't I? Well yes, they can. One thing vampires have really mastered is employing every possible little thing women find attractive. I swear they have a handbook. But I've never known one who couldn't raise one eyebrow and lower the other one in that incredibly hot way. They also lower their chins and look out the tops of their eyes very frequently, which is fine, because that trick *never* gets old. They also wear dress shirts with the cuffs turned up a lot.

Part One:
Dr. Steven Grey/Beyond Bad, to Evil

What makes a person yearn not for a bad vampire, but an evil one?

I confess I was such a person, and why is a complicated matter. I went through a time when my circumstances pushed me in that direction. There was a very demanding and unkind mortal I was dating, and various obligations that pressed me to ignore my own needs too much of the time. I was raised to be good, and I turned that into being a sort of martyr to the demands of others.

Meanwhile, quietly and unobtrusively, my Inner Mina was growing into a sort of monster. Not the kind of monster that you unleash on others; the kind you unleash on yourself. This Monster Mina made me feel like the one thing that could free me from my obsessive devotion to "being good" (read: neglecting myself) was true evil: evil in the form of a powerful, dangerous, sexy vampire.

Enter Dr. Steven Grey.

Dr. Grey is an English professor at a university near where I live, and well-known among mortals as an expert on vampires in literature and pop culture. Contrary to his respectable reputation, Dr. Grey is well-known in the vampire community as a dangerous spokesperson for the Vampire Liberation Movement. The VLM opposes the civilized, benevolent approach to undeadness that most modern vampires espouse. The immortals of my acquaintance consider Dr. Grey as a vampire to be feared and avoided at all costs.

Unfortunately, warnings I received like "stay away from this one" had the opposite effect. They became an irresistible invitation to awake my Monster Mina. When I first encountered Dr. Grey, via the essay you'll read below, I was horrified and fascinated by his words. He was unlike any vampire I knew. I understood why I should stay away from him, but I couldn't. My inner dialogues were running the gamut from rationalizing ("How could anything bad happen to me?") to arrogance ("I know what I'm doing."). He was like a drug that could kill you even on the first try, yet the promise of the thrill is too tempting to set aside. His words made me want to meet him all the more. So read them, if you dare.

THE HIDEOUS DOMESTICATION OF VAMPIRES

By Steven Grey, Ph.D.
(from *Collected Essays on the Vampiric Nature*,
Seth Morgenstern, Ed.)

It cannot be denied that our kind, in recent decades, has been moving toward abandoning our predatory nature. Most of my colleagues look to the development of synthblood as the primary catalyst for this phenomenon, but I see a different mechanism at work. I believe that vampires, nature's most powerful seducers, are themselves being seduced by the modern myth of the undead as romantic heroes.

With the popularization in mortal media of the vampire as protagonist, we find mortal culture developing a more accepting attitude toward our race. We ought to respond by taking advantage, using this new appeal as a tool in the hunt, leveraging it to our benefit as predators. But instead, too many of us now see ourselves as potential heroes, as "romantic leads," if you will.

We use our powers of mesmerization to amuse and entertain our mortal prey. We feed carefully and safely, and only when the victim has given tacit permission. Hunting has become an erotic game for both parties. Lured by the hope of moral redemption, we seek a beneficial place in the lives of mortals. It is not the ready availability of an alternate food source that is to blame, but our aspirations for goodness and the approval of mortalkind.

What a catastrophic situation. I consider myself an articulate man, but I cannot express in words the black rage I feel over this self-inflicted humiliation upon our race.

I call upon my fellow immortals to pause and consider this matter, not with your heads but your hearts and viscera. Have you truly forgotten what it is like to fill your victim with terror, to see her shrink back in mindless fear for her life? Do you not recall the feeling of euphoric power when your will conquers hers, and you see that horror and revulsion turn to fascination and lust? These things are what you were made for, they are your legacy and privilege!

To immobilize a mortal will, then force it to desire your bite above all things . . . to take a creature that once trembled in peril and make it want nothing save to yield its lifeblood to your lips . . . to feel it weaken in your arms even as your strength *is augmented with each draught of hot, rich blood . . . these are the true joys of the vampire, joys to which it is our right and destiny.*

I adjure you, my fellows, look within yourselves and rediscover your truest nature. You were not created to be some sort of erotic toy or guardian angel for whatever mortal attracts your eye. Do not allow this unfortunate trend to upset the proper order of things. It is you who rule, you who control, you who take whatever is your desire.

All you need to confirm this is to recall, in deep and honest detail, what it is like to feed as genuine vampires do: to press your will upon the struggling victim and feel her utter capitulation; to hold her warm and suppliant body in your arms; to pierce her flesh; to feel her start in your embrace as the bliss overcomes her; to suck at your will, slowly or feverishly, tasting every hot, delicious swallow and feeling life roar in your veins.

You were created to do this, to be this — a sublime predator, who cares for nothing but the gratification of his own desires. To be anything else, to temper your nature in the slightest, is blasphemy.

You must be what you are — we all must be what we are — or I fear the predators will in the end be enslaved by their own prey.

I urge you to join me.

chapter 3

Not Just Any Immortal Will Do

if you're like I was at first, you're so excited about the prospect of being with a vampire that you don't particularly care *which* vampire. You've already learned that every one of them is preternaturally perfect, can arch one eyebrow at you, and will stare you into yielding blissfully. So why be picky?

Well, one reason is because picking a cruel one can be fatal, which is why I include the story of Dr. Grey in this book. Not fatal in an "undead-lovers-for-all-eternity" kind of way. . . . I mean fatal in a rip-your-throat-out-so-as-to-exsanguinate-you-faster kind of way. Perversely, the cruel ones are sometimes the sexiest, so choosing an immortal boyfriend takes careful, rational thinking.

Even taking the first *good* vampire that comes along is not your best approach. Because vampire dating and mortal dating have one thing in common: if you want a relationship to last, you need to find someone who is compatible with you. In the case of Ethan, he was best suited for a fellow musician, and the two weeks I spent trying to teach myself the Native American flute didn't quite qualify me.

So as you get to know a vampire, try your best not to be dazzled by what he has to offer. Weigh each skill and character trait objectively. If you broke up with a mortal guy over his obsession with Frisbee golf, you shouldn't be enamored of a vampire because he can throw a Frisbee two thousand feet and hit the "5 JKL" button on a pay phone. If you wouldn't contact a guy through Match.com because he's seeking a literary intellectual, don't stick with a vampire because he can recite all of Shakespeare's sonnets in a deep, resonant voice that makes you feel fluttery inside.

CHEMISTRY IS NOT A GOOD LITMUS TEST

I know this will not be easy. Not all the typical dating rules apply. For example, normally you can go out a couple of times with a guy and determine if you should pursue a relationship by whether or not you feel that "chemistry." Unfortunately, every vampire you meet is going to pour on so much chemistry in the first few minutes that you won't know your CO_2 from your H_2O. He'll "blind you with science," if you will.

Admittedly, this makes it difficult to judge what qualities he has that you like and dislike. Whereas previously you never had use for guys who watch too much baseball, just meet a fanged fan and suddenly you're sighing in ecstasy over recitations of batting averages and ERAs.

But take it from me, eventually his desire to entertain you with MLB stats will wear thin, no matter how seductively executed and with what fine arching of brows it is punctuated.

You must, I repeat, *must* apply reason to the situation.

It helps if you take the same list you prepared to guide you in your selection of mortal mates, and apply it unswervingly to vampires as well. Does your list say you want a guy who is funny, likes cats, can cook, and dance? Then don't give up until you've found a vampire who is funny, likes cats, can cook, and dance. Trust me, there is an immortal out there for you. He is hilarious in a sexy way, owns an ocelot, makes his own sushi, and specializes in the tango. In fact, he has the power to enable you to tango with him perfectly on the first try.

Now aren't you glad you waited for Mr. Right?

SAVE YOUR COMPROMISING FOR YOUR MORTAL RELATIONSHIPS

This brings me to the good news: Seeing as all vampires are over-achievers and flawless and all that, your odds of finding Mr. Right Vampire are much better than finding Mr. Right Mortal. That old saw, "nobody's perfect," applies to the latter. With immortals, use "everybody's perfect," please. When you are seeking a regular boyfriend you will no doubt need to compromise. If he is good with puns and can negotiate a grill, you should probably overlook his preference for dogs.

There is no need to settle for less with vampires. Each and every one of them can be riotously witty if he wants to. Having been around for several centuries at least, they have accumulated a lot more recipes than you, and have had plenty of practice at any kind of dance. So all you need to do, therefore, is not settle for the one with the hellhound and wait for the one with the ocelot.

But you must stick to your guns — and do not leave the discriminating to the vampire. Vampires are typically not picky themselves; as I said, they like people who like vampires, and will find something about you to appreciate no matter what other qualities you bring to the table. Meanwhile, there are a few of them you need to watch out for: vampires who see you as just another potential notch on their coffin. These sorts of undead guys are all about being anything you want them to be — but only until teeth break flesh. Needless to say, that can be a real downer for you.

THE GOOD, THE BAD, AND WELL, ACTUALLY, THERE ARE NO UGLY ONES

I'm betting there are more than a few of you out there who have found yourselves, against your better judgment, wishing to hang out with an evil vampire. It's actually quite common. Sure, we women appreciate those nice, upstanding vampires who struggle valiantly against their primordial urges to suck us dry. But we also get off on the vampires who are perfectly determined to suck us dry, and so much the better if we beg them to.

"So much the better if we beg them to"? Now why the heck do we females get a thrill out of a concept like that? Are we crazy? Can we really get away with just blaming the mind control? Especially when we liked the idea of the mind control even before it kicked in?

I, of all people, can certainly explain. This is just another one of those counterintuitive phenomena like the fact that untethering your Inner Mina results in your having a spine of iron. Your yearning for a bad vampire is not because you are a bad person. It's because you are a *good* person. In fact, almost *too* good.

WHEN YOU'RE TOO GOOD, THINGS GET NASTY

Human society has always been demanding toward women. I don't care whether you're talking about pre-Susan B. Anthony days or right now. We are expected to behave like ladies, be the glue that keeps the family together, and not backstab our way to the top at the office. If a man dumps his wife, buys a Corvette, and takes a month off from work to sew his wild oats, people may gossip about his mid-life crisis, but they will feel he's just being a man. If a woman did those things, her reputation would really take a beating. When men steal, slit throats, and nail any wench they can get their hands on, they are called pirates and people write stories about them. Were a woman to try that, well, she might become a tabloid celebrity if she's hot-looking, but otherwise forget it.

We females are just supposed to be *nice*, that's all. I think there's been one popular woman in history who wasn't nice, and that was Scarlett O'Hara. She's popular with women, anyway, and men only give her a pass because she's sexy. I make my point.

Because we are forced by our culture to be nice whether we feel like it or not, women have had to subjugate their be-a-pirate, Scarlett O'Hara-esque urges to their subconscious minds. That stuff builds up after awhile, and we pretend it's not even there, until finally we are what vampires call — and I'm not making this up —"ready for nasty."

Not "ready for *the* nasty," as in trolling for sex or something. No, I said "ready for nasty."

Women just get so sick of being good that they are completely and utterly and downright chomping-at-the-bit ready for a nasty vampire. And when you are ready for nasty, what you need is a bad vampire.

Please understand, however, what I mean here by "bad vampires." I mean *bad*, which is very different from *evil*. Bad vampires are actually respectable immortals whose personalities tend to the predatory, and are pretty nasty all the time, in a good way. The great thing about vampires is that even the "good" ones, the less predatory ones, can employ nastiness when the occasion requires it. Evil vampires, on the other hand, can actually behave very nicely while luring you into a situation that will not be nasty at all, but rather *very, very bad*.

With this caveat in mind, you shouldn't feel in the least bit ashamed about being ready for nasty. It's not like you want to ditch your boyfriend and join a pirate crew. It's not like you want to flunk out of school, become a blogger or a Vegas escort. In fact, it's not like you want to stop being good or even be *less* good. You simply want to spend some time in the company of a bad vampire, the kind who flies (sometimes literally) in the face of social convention, likes his blood straight-up, and makes no apologies for getting whatever he wants not later but right this f-ing instant, if you please.

You will find that hanging out with a bad vampire goes a long way toward boosting your patience with friends who ignore your texts, incomprehensible professors, and boyfriends who want to watch wrestling every weekend. In fact, the delicious nastiness of these vampires will be the very tonic that enables you to smile at incompetent post

-office clerks, volunteer at soup kitchens, and even get coffee for your Neanderthal boss who doesn't realize 1960s sensibilities are cute on TV but not in real life. Annoying people will still aggravate you (especially when you compare them to the perfection of vampires), but you will tolerate them so much better because you finally have an area of your life where aggression is freely expressed. Am I suggesting you might be picturing the post-office clerk being taught a lesson by your vampire friends? Well, yeah, maybe. . . .

Okay, to go over these categories one final time:

GOOD VAMPIRE: a guy like Ethan, who just wants to charm women into yielding to his bite with his physical beauty and glorious music.

BAD VAMPIRE: a guy like Gunnar, who seduces with his air of threatening menace, but when push comes to shove wouldn't hurt a fly.

EVIL VAMPIRE: Dr. Steven Grey perfectly illustrates this type of vampire.

THE SECRET OF THE RED SATIN RIBBON

Okay, now swear to me that you've got these distinctions clear. I believe we've arrived at the moment when I can safely share with you a very important — but also potentially dangerous — secret.

Many centuries ago, in Eastern Europe where the undead were first discovered, vampires were dreaded and feared. However, one mortal woman — known as Valeria in legend — dared to consort with immortals. She fell in love with the vampire Trajan, who had been a soldier of great heroism in his mortal life. Knowing the displeasure the relationship would cause her family if discovered, Valeria and Trajan went to great lengths to keep their love a secret. Often, after sunset, Valeria would go to the marketplace and wear a red satin ribbon tied to her wrist. The ribbon was a signal to Trajan that she could meet him later that evening outside the walls of the city.

Unfortunately, Valeria's younger sister, Magda, learned of the lover's bond. Wanting to attract an immortal of her own, Magda began wearing a red satin ribbon on her wrist. She accidently let the reason why be overheard by the city's chief, a zealous vampire hater. The chief hunted down Valeria and sentenced her to be burned at the stake for consorting with evil.

Valeria wore her ribbon to her execution to proclaim her faithfulness to Trajan. And the vampire was just as faithful to his mortal true love: he had been watching over her throughout the proceedings. No sooner was the fire lit beneath Valeria's feet, when Trajan leapt through the flames to be at her side. He lovingly caressed her cheek. Then triumphantly, before all in attendance, Trajan converted Valeria so she could be with him forever.

Ever since that time, those who love vampires have dared to wear the red satin ribbon to express their clandestine feelings to immortals who may happen upon them. For obvious reasons, the meaning has been passed secretly, with the utmost care, from one vampirophile to another over the centuries.

Much more recently, in the past two hundred years or so, a second custom has arisen. Those extreme vampire lovers who are enamored of their evil aspects employ a slight variation and wear the ribbon on their left (aka "sinister," in the ancient meaning of that word) wrist. This is, in my opinion, a very dangerous practice. It may be a titillating thought to invite an evil vampire's attentions, but those sorts of immortals are not watching out for you like Trajan did for Valeria. To them the red satin ribbon is more like a garnish, if you follow my meaning.

That said, if you truly want to proclaim your interest in the undead *to* the undead, what you need to do is this: wear a red satin ribbon tied around your wrist. It must be red, not pink or black or puce. It must be satin, not velvet, not raffia, not paper or plastic. And it must be a ribbon, not a cord or a string or a tattoo of a ribbon. I know these are very specific requirements, but it is essential that you follow them to a T. And tie the ribbon in a bow, like on a shoelace. A double knot is fine.

Now that you know, I must rush in with my big caveat: even if you employ the safer right wrist, wear with care. Do not put on the red satin ribbon carelessly. Because it gets results. And as you will learn in the chapters that follow, sometimes they are not the results you are looking for.

But let's not end this chapter on such an alarming note. The red satin ribbon has its risks, but it is also a real boon to those who employ it wisely. It can do a lot to help you catch the perfect vampire, ready for nasty or not.

Case Study 103:

*Me, Mordred, and Adam, and how
I almost picked the wrong vampire.*

Mordred and Adam are best friends. I'm not sure about the back story on that, but you'd never meet a pair of guys more dissimilar. Mordred has a much more conventional vampire look happening: dark brown hair, sexy beard neatly trimmed, eyes the color of black coffee, and a fondness for wearing black leather gloves at all times. He has never told me his age or heritage, preferring to keep it a mystery. I imagine him being born in the Dark Ages, and being a practitioner of druidic arts who fell in with the wrong crowd and ended up undead, much to his own satisfaction. I've wondered if perhaps that's precisely his story, and he actually put the idea in my head.

Adam, on the other hand, looks like someone from The Shire, only taller and thinner and without pointed ears. He is puckish, cute, and has red hair and olive green eyes. Someone not paying attention would never pick him for a vampire, but if you were on the lookout — which I always am, of course — you'd recognize the undead in him. That "cute" I mention is the kind of cute that makes you want to let him eat you up, not vice-versa.

I met these two one night in a club where they invited me to play pool. I teamed with Adam against Mordred. It was clear from the get-go that they were both toying with me, and I expected nothing less, since I knew from experience they were vampires. Adam's way of toying with me was much nicer than Mordred's. He kept telling me how good my shots were, and giving me tips, and rewarding me, even when I scratched, with a gentle word and a pat on the back. A pat on the back from a vampire is a very nice thing.

Mordred toyed with me by deliberately missing shots. And he

remained absolutely silent as we played, focusing completely on the game, not even acknowledging that I was there. Except that while Adam was shooting, I'd look over at Mordred leaning against a pillar, and find his black eyes trained upon me with a look that made my knees weak.

Mordred seemed the sort of vampire that should not be my type, in that my type was not lethal and quietly, sexily deranged (or so I told myself). I was convinced that if I found myself alone with him, he would either convert me immediately or simply drain me to death. And yet, oddly, I continued to try to catch him looking at me. Just to see if it made my knees weak every time, which of course it did. And those leather gloves. . . .

I am not particularly good at pool, and Adam was more interested in encouraging me than winning, and Mordred kept deliberately missing, so the game went on for quite awhile. The last six balls seemed unwilling to enter the pockets. Finally, without a word, Mordred leaned over the table (a pose that I assure you took my breath away), aimed his cue nonchalantly, and hit a combo shot that sunk every remaining ball, the eight ball last.

He stood up, holding the cue in one gloved hand as if it were in fact a rapier, and stared at me.

"Well done," I squeaked.

He nodded, a silent salute.

"Diana," said Adam, "do you feel like some late-night tacos?"

I said yes, and Mordred bid us farewell. Literally, just one word: "Farewell."

At the taco place, Adam proved to be even nicer than Ethan had been. He had been born in Scotland in the 19th century, and told me about the lochs with words both vivid and sentimental. He joked that Nessie the monster had been a personal friend. His green eyes were gorgeous and hypnotic, and he had a heartwarming smile. When Adam kissed me goodnight, it was exactly like I imagined kisses would be like when I was young and only knew about romance from the movies. He took my face in his hands, I closed my eyes, I heard the violins swell and felt my heart brim with joy, and when his lips caressed mine it seemed like a chorus was singing a glorious chord. He was a vampire, yes, but the very, very sweet kind. So sweet in fact that I prayed his mouth would slip down my neck from that kiss, and by his bite fill my blood with that same sweetness. Alas, he did not bite me that first evening. Adam was, shall I say, quite good.

During this time I was working as a legal secretary in a big downtown firm. I'd been to college and was well-read and therefore thought that with time and hard work I could advance professionally at the firm. Unfortunately, my bosses preferred to keep me simply typing and filing.

I would meet Adam for dinner and he always lent a sympathetic ear. It did help to have someone to gripe to, but not much. The weeks passed and I just couldn't figure out how to adjust my attitude to make my job more endurable. Things came to a head when I was passed over for a promotion. I was so mad I called Adam, but he really didn't know what to say to me.

Later that afternoon, I answered my phone and heard a strange voice on the line.

"Adam is not going to help you," it said.

Could it really be Mordred? But it had to be; no one else I knew had such a menacing, low voice. "Mordred?" I said into the phone, trying not to let my voice tremble.

"Yes," he replied. "*I'm* going to help you."

When I got home from work that day he was waiting on my

front porch, again leaning against a pillar. I could tell by looking at him that were it not for the custom of waiting to be invited in, he would have been waiting in the living room, perhaps coiled and ready to spring. I invited him in.

Why did I invite him in when I was terrified of him? At the time I was absolutely baffled, but I can explain it now: my frustrations at work had made me very ready for nasty.

Mordred waited until I'd set down my purse before gripping my shoulders in his gloved hands and pinning me to the wall of the foyer. "Why did you choose Adam?" he asked, his eyes blazing.

"He seemed nice," I managed to reply. The painful grip of his fingers on my shoulders and the piercing fury in his eyes made me fear for my life.

"He *is* nice, and you're a fool," said Mordred.

By the time he finished kissing me, I had to agree with him.

He didn't bite me that night, although I was sure until the moment he departed my doorway that he was going to. But I learned the man actually has quite old-fashioned principles, for all his propensity for violence.

The next morning, to my shock, Mordred came to the law firm. He met briefly with one of my bosses behind closed doors. After he left — of course with only a dark glance toward my desk — my boss called me into his office, apologized for being a jerk, and invited me to lunch.

It was much easier than I expected to explain to Adam that I was leaving him for Mordred. He just grinned and said, "See, I knew you were simply too good for me."

Too good . . . I had to think about it awhile, but then I realized exactly what he meant by that.

FAQS ABOUT THE UNDEAD

Q: I thought vampires subsisted on blood alone; why then would they collect recipes and know how to make sushi?

A: I don't know why everyone persists in thinking vampires don't eat and drink regular stuff as well as blood. Seriously, where's the logic? Vampires are no different than you and I in this regard. Mortals don't need to consume vanilla cherry cola and malted milk balls to *survive*, but they partake of them anyway.

Q: If all vampires are perfect, can they all hit the "5 JKL" button on a pay phone with a Frisbee?

A: Vampires *are* all perfect, but they are not all equivalent. Whatever a vampire is into, he's into it completely. A vampire may be better at pool than his friend, because he likes the game more than the friend and applies himself to the skill. One vampire may have memorized the entire contents of the Internet Movie Database, while another beats all comers at whist. That said, there are plenty of skills all vampires share in common and do well, like mind control and remaining extremely pale.

Q: You talk about "good" vampires. I thought all vampires had lost their souls, so how does that work?

A: It's actually not possible to "lose your soul" without ceasing to be a member of the human species. Vampires may be immortal, but they are still quite human. There's simply been a campaign throughout history to convince everyone that vampires are damned, I'm not a historian so I can't tell you how that got started, but I personally feel it's just that there's always someone who has to be a buzzkill. Anyway, knowing this will be a point in your favor when you try to connect with a vampire; they are always pleased to meet people who don't think they're damned.

chapter 4

Vampire Catching Tips
(Don't Hunt After Eating Scampi)

I know in this book I've been blowing away many of your cherished, long-held beliefs about vampire lore. And while a lot of that is just stuff-and-nonsense, a few of the rumors are true. For example, most vampires do detest garlic, so ordering shrimp scampi on your dinner date may be a *faux pas*. On the other hand, like I said earlier, I've met a couple immortals who like garlic shrimp, so you never can tell.

My point is, based on conventional wisdom about blood-drinkers, you are not necessarily going to know what to do and where to go. When I first got into the game, I made a lot of mistakes because I took my cues from the clichés. It wasn't until I starting thinking outside the oblong box, if you will, that I had success meeting vampires.

THERE'S A LIGHT OVER AT THE FRANKENSTEIN PLACE

For starters, let's say I asked you where you might go to find immortals hanging out. What would you say? Transylvania? Scary old castles? Of course not; but still, you'd probably think along the lines of the modern day equivalent of such Gothic locales. Perhaps your local creepy Halloween corn maze, or a Knights of Columbus Haunted House? Tattoo parlors, Goth bars? A Buffy convention? The midnight theater showing *Rocky Horror Picture Show*?

If you approach the challenge this way, you won't get far. You're limiting yourself to the obvious, and vampires are never obvious. Stop and think about the places I've mentioned where I encountered immortals. A *mall food court*? A *laundromat*? Who would have guessed? Well, that's my point: vampires can be anywhere and everywhere. Your first instruction is *don't rule out any possibility*. It's like this: vampires love to be in settings where they can shine, and they can shine in any setting.

You just need to look for the shine.

Yes, that statement right there is my best advice to you. Wherever you go, whatever you do, be on the lookout for the shine. The shine is that glorious thing about the guy across the room that makes your heart skip and sing. You might find it in some specific feature: the color of his eyes, the way he walks, an interesting remark he makes like "listen, the stars are whispering" (that was Sven). Or maybe you can't put your finger on it — his presence just seems to fill the room and take hold of you. Perhaps, like you learned from my story about Ethan, no one else will pay him any notice. But for you, it will feel like walking into a wall. A nice, tingly, heavenly wall.

Now, let's say you've spotted this vampire. His shine has fairly knocked you unconscious, but then the bus comes, or he disappears into an elevator, or his girlfriend shows up and kisses him. While this will of course prevent you from pursuing that particular guy, don't despair. I've found that even these brief encounters with vampires can make a person's whole day. Feel free to think about him wistfully for as long as you like, or concoct nice daydreams in which he feeds upon you in various delightful ways. That kind of thing can be quite satisfying in its own right.

THE VAMPIRE'S "CHECKLIST"

But let's say he's alone, and he notices you. What can you do to appeal to a vampire, besides, of course, sporting the red satin ribbon?

You might not be the prettiest girl in the cereal aisle; maybe along with the ribbon on your wrist, you're wearing tooth-whitening strips and sweats. Why should he show *you* any particular attention?

Happily for all of us, and contrary to the movies where all the vampire victims are gorgeous, blood-drinkers are not like mortal guys and can actually see past the epidermis. Whether you're A-pos, or B-neg, or anything in between, it's possible for *anyone* to have what vampires are looking for.

(And, by the way, the subtly different tastes of blood types are discernible to the undead: they all have their preferences, and AB-neg is quite a culinary delicacy.)

And just what, exactly, does the typical vampire include on his checklist? He wants a girl who:

1. Believes in vampires. Now don't just laugh this off as obvious; it really means a lot. Let's say you landed on a planet where hardly anyone believed in women . . . where everyone kept saying, "You're not a woman, there are no such things as women." Suddenly you encounter somebody who looks at you and says, "Oh wow! A real woman! This is awesome!" Nice.

2. Appreciates the shine. Although no one can resist a vampire, it's also true that some appreciate the sensual, seductive, mysterious, magical allure of vampires more than others. And you know who you are.

3. Has no particular expectations. Each vampire is an individual treasure trove of treats, and he wants to be appreciated for his unique gifts. Nothing quells the undead *joie de vivre* more quickly than someone demanding the clichés. "Where's your cape?" "Shouldn't you have *black* hair?" "What's with the Yiddish accent?" Mood killers.

4. Is ready for nasty. In the case of bad vampires. In the case of nice ones, see #3.

5. Is yielding. I mean that in more than the obvious way. Certainly regarding the obvious way, any vampire can get "yielding" out of any victim. I'm talking about the more subtle kinds of yielding, like yielding your imagination, your state of mind, your outlook.

SHOW HIM YOU'RE THAT *SPECIAL* KIND OF "VICTIM"

So there you are, huddling in a bus shelter on a rainy night, when a fellow in one of those cool ankle-length trench coats suddenly joins you. Your eyes meet, he says "Good evening." What should you do to make the most of the moment?

In my experience, the great thing about vampires is they are happy to take the lead. You're never going to get a "I dunno, what movie do *you* wanna see?" out of a vampire. (It's really quite refreshing.) So it's a lot like ballroom dancing when your partner is Fred Astaire. All you really have to do is follow, and vampires being vampires, your immortal will most certainly see that you do.

This doesn't mean there's absolutely no need for you to exert yourself. Keep in mind that, seeing as vampires can get any girl to surrender, they are quite adept at telling one kind of surrender from another. Interestingly, they generally prefer those who surrender proactively.

Obviously that statement bears elaboration.

Let's say your blood-loving friend is sitting on a sofa with you in front of a crackling fire, telling you one of his mystical stories that start out as a sort of fairy tale/bedtime story and end up revealing some profundity about your life. (This is a typical vampire date activity, actually.) He won't really mind if you just sit there holding his pleasantly cool hand and listening. But he'll like it much better if you let yourself be so caught up in what he's describing to you that you say things like, "So, the flaming bird that's floating in the air before us, Arthur, is it singing?"

Alternatively, perhaps he's taken you flying. (Or convinced you to *believe* you're flying, wink wink.) Sure, he'll settle for a woman who clings to him and cries, "Don't let me fall, oh please don't let me fall!" But he'll much prefer one who looks down and laughs and says, "Oh Maximilian, this is amazing! — whoa, is that the Chrysler Building?"

In short, vampires love swoony women with spunk.

JUST A LITTLE NIP FOR NOW, PLEASE

Which brings us to one final thought concerning that first encounter. You may think the question completely moot, but it's important to decide going in just how far you are willing to go, bite-wise, in this particular circumstance. I just don't want you to come away from your vampire date feeling like you let things get out of hand.

. . . *follow me to page 70*

top ten vampire pickup lines

Sure, vampires can seduce with a glance. But for fun, they sometimes emulate mortals and try out pickup lines. Here are my personal favorites.

1. *The nice:* "Your irresistible loveliness called to me from across this Jiffy Lube waiting room."

2. *The nasty:* "It's exquisite how badly you long for my bite — I think I'll just wait awhile until you beg me for it" (accompanied by fierce and sexy glare).

3. *The romantic:* "They say a diamond is forever — I can promise you an eternity."

4. *The funny:* "I'd love to kiss those rosebud lips, but if you want a hug afterward it will cost you another bite."

5. *The funny but cheap:* "I picked these flowers up for you . . . at the cemetery."

6. *The silent:* The little beckoning hand gesture that Frank Langella used in the 1979 *Dracula* movie. Hand is down at side, slight, slow twist of the wrist. Sigh . . .

7. *The cocky:* "I can be your Lestat, your Edward, your Bill . . . only even better."

8. *The masterful:* "You will come to me now — you must come to me — and you will yield to me your soul" (accompanied by penetrating stare you can feel down to your toes).

9. *The bilingual:* "Donnez-moi votre sang, ma chérie, maintenant" (simply means "give me your blood, my dear, now," but isn't the French sexier?).

10: *The classic charmer:* "Look deep, deep into my eyes." So simple, but never fails.

By the way, you will never hear any vampire say, "I see you're my type: O-positive." They are just not that uncool.

There are actually very few vampires out there evil enough to want to drain or convert a girl with his first bite, so odds are good you're not in any danger of being killed or turned into a vampire. Still, being bitten is a pretty extreme experience, and one can be hurt by getting so intimate and transcendent right away. You might choose to wait till you know him a little better, or you can let him have a little nip so you can see what his bite is like. Or, if you're sure, you can throw all caution to the wind and let him take a full pint.

By the way, today's vampires are very good at judging how much a pint is, and they actually seldom drink that much at a sitting. If your vampire does, you'll have another test of whether he's good or bad: the good ones will give you some orange juice after, and probably a cookie. They want the experience to be safe for you.

I may have thrown you off a bit here. After all, I've been talking for pages and pages about how vampires are going to get their way with you whether you like it or not. So now, just when we've gotten to the nitty-gritty, why am I suggesting you can just tell him you'd prefer to pass?

Well, this is one of the most interesting things about vampires: Most of them truly do respect a woman's blood. I'm sure things were different back in the days before synthblood, when a starving immortal could hardly be expected to ignore that succulent, pulsing little blue vein barely concealed by a high lace collar. But nowadays, they can afford to be more subtle and conniving and deliciously slow about their seductions.

It's just more fun for everyone that way.

Case Study 104:

Me, Colin, and how I decided to pass on the bite.

Colin is one of the most fascinating vampires I've ever met. He was born in Jamaica in the late 1700s, the child of African slaves on a coffee plantation, and was converted when he was 26. He lived through quite interesting times — the Maroon War, the Baptist War, the freeing of the slaves and the Apprentice System — well, suffice it to say, he operated as a vampire in all sorts of situations, and before the advent of synthblood, too.

He took the name Colin much later in life, in the 1980s, when he started working on his doctoral dissertation on vampires in literature at Oxford. By that time he'd studied vampires from a number of viewpoints for going on two centuries, so as you might guess, it was a controversial but quite impressive dissertation.

I met Colin, fittingly, in a library. He was sitting in a secluded corner reading, less fittingly, *The Tale of Peter Rabbit*.

I recognized him for what he was at once, and found his choice of reading material intriguing. So I sat down in the chair next to his, waited for him to look at me, and asked softly, "Peter Rabbit?"

"Right. Yes. Well, I've never read it," he replied, in an equally unexpected British accent. "Came out in 1902, you know, and I stopped being age appropriate in 1790 or so."

"So, why are you reading it now?"

"A friend suggested it was a good reminder of what it's like to get in trouble for eating what one shouldn't," he replied.

I laughed quietly, and was completely charmed, without him even having to charm me supernaturally. I should mention that he was elegantly handsome, with the most wonderfully arched nostrils and flawless brown skin. Colin was my first vampire of color, and I confess it was fascinating to meet a vampire who wasn't white as snow.

We went out for tea, and that night he made me a Jamaican-style dinner with jerk chicken and rum-raisin ice cream, and I bombarded him with questions about vampires (many of the same ones you see in my FAQs in this book), which he answered patiently. He had a gentle way of speaking but a hearty and musical laugh. He seemed to know everything in the world, and imparted his knowledge in the most entertaining ways.

Colin's understanding of seduction and submission was intellectually brilliant. I responded to it on that level, intellectually, but also on a more, shall we say, "visceral" level. Between his gorgeously exotic nose, his accent, and that marvelous mind, I really, really wanted him to bite me almost immediately.

But you know what? I asked him not to.

If you've been bitten by a vampire you will know what it is like to have your will drain out of you in a rush, leaving you a ragdoll of happy submission. In such a state a person forgets about things like intellectual curiosity and the invigorating exchange of ideas. I enjoyed picking Colin's brain so much, I didn't want to lose interest in that and fritter my first date with him away by lying on his couch blissfully comatose. There might, I hoped, be time for that later . . . but I was too caught up in the thrill of being with such a fascinating person to want to waste it.

FAQS ABOUT THE UNDEAD

Q: Can you explain about vampire fangs?

A: Ah, you mean how vampires look perfectly normal until the biting urge comes upon them, and then — sproing! — their incisors get all pointy? That's how it is in the movies, and interestingly, in real life, too. I'm not sure how they do that exactly, but it's a good thing or they'd scare off all the dentists. Ha ha. Yeah, vampires don't need dentists, obviously — their teeth are just as immortal as the rest of them.

Q: And do their eyes go all weird like some mutant albino cat's eyes you see so often in the movies?

A: Not really. They just peer into yours in a way that makes everything else go dim, and it feels like your soul is being drawn out of you to mingle with theirs, and music seems to float on their gaze right into your brain. The albino cat contacts like the kind that actors wear are just supposed to convey that, I guess. I have to say, the fake lenses totally fail at it.

Q: You said when a person becomes a vampire, he loses the melanin in his skin. How then can there be black vampires like Colin?

A: No one is sure why, but dark-skinned races do not lose *all* their melanin . . . they just lighten up somewhat. In the early 19th century, Colin used to tell people he was a mulatto and that satisfied them. But not too long after that, those talented vampire scientists developed a chemical solution to the problem, an "elixir" that darkened the skin. In fact, Caucasian vampires who eschew the pale look use it, too. Nowadays, you can get synthblood with the darkening agent added if you want (nicknamed "chocolate milk" by some).

Part Two:
Dr. Steven Grey/His Murderous Past

After I read Dr. Steven Grey's menacing essay, I couldn't stop thinking about him. Here was a vampire totally absorbed with the selfish pursuit of human blood, whose carnivorous lust was undiluted by human feelings. I'm ashamed to admit the depraved thrill I got from picturing what such a being would be like; I imagined he had to be more tempting, more enthralling than any vampire I'd ever met. I had to know more, and I began to research the story of Dr. Grey.

I found out the professor hadn't always been a respectable academic . . . as a mortal, he was a serial killer. In late 19th-century Chicago, he committed six brutal murders in which he hung his still-living victims by their feet, cut their throats, and drained them of blood. Why haven't we heard about these horrifying crimes? History doesn't remember Steven Grey because that's the way he wanted it. Very early in his crime spree, Grey made the acquaintance of a vampire.

Recognizing that being undead had its benefits, Grey sought out a vampire to convert him. Once he possessed the immortal's ability to mesmerize, he infiltrated the Chicago Police Department and saw to it that all evidence and records of the murders he committed were destroyed.

And, of course, as a vampire Steven Grey had unlimited ability to seduce, and an even more rewarding way of draining his prey of their blood.

As the years passed, he tired of his hobby of chaotic

destruction. He was too intelligent and crafty to be satisfied by a boring career of serial homicide. So he turned his ambitions to advancing vampires to greater power in the world. He became an academic in the mortal sphere, striving by his position to perpetuate mortals' interest in undeadkind. He also took up speaking and writing for the vampire audience, trying to win them to his point of view.

Meanwhile, I learned, Dr. Grey made it his own particular challenge to make trouble for vampires and mortals alike: trouble that was often worse than mere death. His "specialty" was deceiving people into making terrible mistakes, then converting them, so they would spend eternity wracked by guilt and regret. For example, he loved to mesmerize women into murdering their own husbands, just before making them undead. No sooner would such a new vampire emerge from the ecstasy of conversion, then she would discover her last act as a mortal had been to stab or shoot or drown her dearest love.

Such information was not lost on me. I recognized Steven Grey was surely a monster, but I couldn't let go of my perverse fascination.

I went online and looked up Steven Grey, Ph.D., professor of English, on the university's Web site.

I found his picture. Grey was an appropriate name indeed, for he had salt-and-pepper hair, and dark gray eyes under black brows. He looked intelligent, worldly-wise, and distinguished. He was blindingly handsome. And I swore to myself I could recognize, deep in his eyes, a murderous, seductive gleam.

I became all the more determined to meet him.

chapter 5

If I Decide to Let Him Bite Me — Then What?

to those of you who by this point have caught yourselves a vampire, congratulations are in order. This is because, to adapt an old saying, "you don't choose a vampire, he chooses you." If you find yourself in the enviable position of dating an immortal, rest assured you earned it.

You've completed the catching . . . now it's time to learn about the keeping.

There are many considerations to keeping a vampire, but one of them needs to be addressed first: this business of bites. You may have wanted to wait at first, but eventually the right time will come. Obviously dating a vampire and not letting him bite you is akin to dating a masseuse and never getting a shiatsu. What's the point of the fangs if you never let them sink in?

So, let's assume you've found a vampire you feel you can trust (or play at distrusting) and you've made the rational (or pretend impulsive) decision to let him bite. Certainly there must be a few things a girl ought to know before that piercing moment occurs.

ONE BITE DOES NOT A VAMPIRE MAKE

There are stages to the process, and they are not like what you've seen in the movies. You may think it goes something like this: First the vampire mesmerizes you; then he bites you, making you his slave; then he bites you again and again over a period of days, during which you become weaker and weaker, eventually becoming bedridden; and then the capper, you run your tongue over your teeth and they've gone pointy.

First of all, as I've explained, any vampire can completely captivate any mortal at will. He wants you — he's got you. But an immortal can choose to spellbind someone with a totally different intent than blood-drinking. Perhaps he simply wants to steal the cab you just hailed. Your being enthralled does not, in and of itself, mean a bite is imminent. Nor is the entranced condition permanent.

Secondly, your first actual bite is not the kiss of death. It doesn't seal some unholy and irrevocable contract between you and the vampire. The one concern you should have is that you will really like it. Above and beyond everything else in your life. To the point of putting your computer in a closet, setting your DVR to record all your shows for the next week, and begging him to feed every night.

I'd like to insert a little tip here. Never do anything drastic like DVR all your shows when you've only been bitten one time. The story is always the same: that first bite feels so much more wonderful than anything that's ever happened to you, you're terrified that maybe it can't be repeated. Rest assured, it can and will be. Take a breath, chill, and wait until after your second bite. You'll realize your initial eagerness to quit Facebook and cancel Netflix was an overreaction.

AND THE BITE GOES ON

Okay, so as your relationship with your vampire continues, you will indeed start feeling yourself getting sucked in. So to speak. Sorry. This is not so much because the vampire bite (even a neck bite) is addictive, physically or psychologically. It's just that the repetition of that kind of intimacy leads to a bond. It's not unlike sex, really. I know our culture tries its darndest to portray sex as no big deal, but in fact anytime a person does something intimate and secret-ey over and over with another person, they're going to end up with a bond, for good or ill.

Repeated bites are not going to weaken you like poor bedridden Mina in the movies. You can, in fact, carry on quite well with your regularly scheduled life if you balance things properly (more on that later). You will not slowly turn immortal as the feedings continue. Your will won't atrophy, turn black, and fall out. You will just be you, only with a secret life in which the guy you're dating drinks your blood.

That all sounds quite lovely, but I must warn you. The more involved you become with your vampire, the more you will inevitably find yourself considering conversion. But that's a whole other topic for later. It's a big enough deal to get its own chapter. I just wanted *you* to know that *I* know you're already wondering about that. For the time being, though, let's take the process one pint at a time.

DON'T TAKE A DARK NATURE TOO LIGHTLY

Which brings me to another caveat. Any concern you have about exsanguination, e.g., being drained of blood, is not unreasonable. Synthblood or no, a vampire is a wild creature and in a very real sense you are his food. Just like a well-fed tiger is still a tiger, a vampire should be respected as much as any of your untamed carnivores. That said, modern vampires are mindful of maintaining good P.R. and as a society they really don't condone leaving a lot of bloodless corpses in their wake. Only the meanest, craziest of them will set upon you with the intent of draining you into oblivion.

Sometimes, however, the best-laid plans of vampires go awry (as you will learn in the Case Study to follow). For this reason you must really try, in spite of the swirly eyes and the blissful rush of ecstasy in your bloodstream, to keep this mantra in the forefront of your mind: "He mustn't drink it all." Seriously, for your own safety, repeat after me: "He mustn't drink it all." Holding this thought is no guarantee, but it can really get you out of a jam. Think of it as a vampiric seatbelt.

how to say no to a vampire

It may surprise you to learn that in many circumstances, you can actually refuse a vampire. My friend Angela learned how from an authority, and is delighted to share the technique.

One day after work I found a note tucked under the wiper of my car. It said, "Dear Vampirophile Angela, you have been selected for a private session on a topic of your choice regarding the customs of the undead. Your instructor will be Horatio. Payment, in the amount of one pint, will be due at the end of the session. See you after sunset."

A pint of blood was a small price to pay for what I wanted Horatio to teach me: how to say no to a vampire.

My teacher first made it clear that when a mortal is in thrall to a vampire, saying no is simply not an option. However, any time you are engaged in normal conversation with an immortal, it is perfectly possible to refuse him something . . . but you really, really must do it according to proper protocol. Here's what Horatio told me:

1. Set your spirit in a deferential mode. The vampire will sense that you recognize you are at his mercy. This will make him more likely to indulge you.

2. Express your wish to decline and the reason therefore. Be direct and succinct.

3. Do not whine or grovel. If you wish to refer to your vampire as "my lord" or "master," you may, but do so with self-assurance.

4. Wait for his reaction with optimism. The undead like to feel that their victims trust in their good will and affection, and are not cringing, waiting for the axe (or fangs) to fall.

5. Say thank you when he accepts your "no."

Horatio took his payment, and then observed that drinking a second pint of my blood would be very nice. I bowed my head respectfully, told him no, my lord, two pints would possibly kill me, and I smiled. He responded with a grin and said I'd passed the final exam. I looked up and said thank you.

IT'S ABOUT SO MUCH MORE THAN THE BLOOD

Now with all our considerations of a vampire's motivation, we haven't really addressed how you, the victim, may react to your new relationship with a blood-drinker. Everyone worries about the *vampire* being shallow, the *vampire* being in it only for the feeding. In fact, the incidence of mortals being the ones who only care about the blood is higher than the vampires. It's a novelty and a thrill for *you*; he's probably been doing this for centuries. His interest in drinking your blood is probably quite personal. He's honestly into *you*.

So try to be sensitive to that. If you don't care what vampire is biting you as long as there are fangs in your neck, he will pick up on that. And he's not going to like it. While I'm not saying he will definitely show his displeasure, remember what I said about untamed carnivores. Besides, would you like it done to you?

The blood-sucking part is thrilling, I'm not going to lie. But believe me, having a genuine relationship with a vampire is even better.

So if you really want to have something serious with your immortal, be aware of the pitfalls I've listed here. Don't be so distracted by the splendor of his bite so that you forget everything he has to offer as a person. Keep talking, keep doing things together, show him he doesn't need to drink from you to make you happy. Be his friend as well as his victim. He'll respond by recognizing this is more than a fly-by-night affair, and be willing to share more of himself with you. You'll find there is quite a lot to know about a centuries-old being, and much of it is fascinating.

One final, simple tip for once you are in the blood-drinking stage: Don't forget to have fun.

Case Study 105:

Michelle, Jesse, and a close call with exsanguination.

Movies and TV shows would lead you to believe that it's the old vampires who are the most dangerous, with their accumulation of power and crafty wiles gained over the centuries. The reality is, you should be a lot more careful around *new* vampires, as my friend Michelle learned all too well. When she met Jesse, he was only a few months past his conversion; she ought to have been terrified.

Michelle was on a run one day through a large park not far from her home. It was very early in the morning, just after dawn, and the place was pretty quiet. But as she jogged around the bend of a wooded path leading to a picnic area, she came upon an interesting sight. There was a young man was seated on the bench of a picnic table, playing guitar, and around him on the grass was an assortment of creatures. There were a few gray squirrels, some robins, some sparrows, a couple of chipmunks, and even a modest-size turtle, all stock-still and staring at the musician.

Michelle stopped running and approached. As remarkable as it was to see a little menagerie of woodland creatures behaving for all the world like they were concertgoers, it was Jesse who held her attention. He had rich brown hair, and the kind of curls that are large and soft and make you desperate to touch them. His eyes were emerald green, the same color as the grass. He had one of those faces that you know would be beautiful on a woman, but is still somehow perfectly masculine.

And his guitar playing! Michelle was transfixed by the beauty of it. She sat down on the grass with the animals and listened. After Jesse finished his song, he set aside his guitar on the picnic table, rose, and walked over to where she was sitting. He knelt in the grass before her and looked hard and long into her eyes; so hard and long she was certain he was taking something out of her with his stare. Then he resumed his seat on the bench, took up the guitar, and began to play again.

What Jesse played turned out to be Michelle's favorite songs for guitar. He played a couple of her most beloved flamenco guitar songs. He played the old folk tune, *The Water Is Wide*, and he played a hard, pounding version of *Hazy Shade of Winter*. She sat very still, barely breathing, hanging on every note. But as she listened so intently, inside her there were frightening forces building up.

The final song Jesse played was *Classical Gas*. If you are not familiar with this song, I recommend you go listen to it online so you can understand what an amazing thing it is. Mason Williams had one hit song, and I think he used up all the genius in his body creating this one incredible piece of music.

Jesse took this extraordinary song and increased its magic tenfold.

Michelle was paralyzed by the wonder of it . . . and inside her there swelled such a bubbling, seething torrent of desire that she was sure she would explode before he finished. When Jesse played the final chords, minor resolving into major, his instrument grew silent, Michelle gasped for breath . . . and she reached for Jesse and he for her, and they collapsed together onto the grass where the animals had previously been gathered.

Jesse buried his face in her neck and bit.

The wild fury inside Michelle was soothed, little by little, with each swallow he took. Unfortunately, the music continued to play in her head, and that served to bolster the fire even as Jesse quenched it.

Michelle's only coherent thought was that she was losing her mind. Everything else was a jumbled swirl of his arms clinging to her, his cool face growing warm against her neck, the feeling she was turning inside out slowly and pleasurably, squirrels, that music, and the mantra that I had taught her to employ in emergencies like this. Except something had gone wrong, and it had turned into "He must drink it all, he must drink it all."

Was Michelle really utterly oblivious to her peril? No, not utterly. Deep down inside her, under all the fire and bliss and surrender, her reason struggled to be heard. It was well aware that the mouth of a deadly predator clung to her neck, swiftly draining her of blood. It knew that she was dying fast. And, terrifyingly, it knew she was totally uninterested in preventing it.

Jesse told me later how it was for him, being with Michelle. As he fed, with each swallow he could feel her happiness grow. It was intoxicating to be able to please someone so, and he had always been the kind who likes to make others happy. Of course, he had been taught by the vampire who converted him, a woman named Sheila, that one oughtn't keep drinking too long. But the problem was that whenever Jesse slowed, he sensed Michelle's fear that he might stop. He didn't want to upset her when it was possible to keep making her so happy.

And then he tapped in, psychically speaking, to her raw and unbridled craving to have every drop of herself end up inside of him. This proved to be more than a vampire of a few months could handle. So, in a matter of less than a minute, both Jesse and Michelle experienced a sensation like falling in love a hundred times all at once. And both of them knew if they stopped what they were doing, it was going to go away.

Of course, for Michelle, that glorious feeling (and everything else about life) was about to go away, anyway.

Fortunately, who should come up the wooded path at that moment but Sheila. From the fact that Michelle was as pale as a vampire by this time, whereas Jesse was pink-cheeked and perky, she saw in an instant what had transpired. She clapped her hands next to Jesse's ear and woke him up from his feeding frenzy. The two of them scooped up Michelle and rushed her to Sheila's house.

As you might imagine, Jesse and Michelle were hardly the first people to get into such a jam. Sheila, meanwhile, was one of those very practical and cautious vampires, who happens to keep transfusion equipment on hand for just such emergencies. Synthblood functions just fine in mortals, regardless of blood type, so in an hour or two Michelle was right as rain . . . although terrified out of her mind, of course.

She wasn't terrified of Jesse, she was terrified of the combination of herself and Jesse. There is nothing more dangerous than a couple whose less desirable tendencies feed off each other. Or, to take a more responsible approach to the problem, let's word it like this: If my attitudes and actions enable the other person's mistreatment of me to continue unabated, I need to (a) change or (b) get away from him.

In the case of Michelle and Jesse, Sheila opted for (b). She's a very wise old vampire, that one.

FAQS ABOUT THE UNDEAD

Q: Are vampires always cold to the touch?

A: A low body temperature, which feels cool to our 98.6-ness, is normal for vampires. However, when they feed, their bodies warm up, sometimes to a temperature that could kill a mortal person. There are practical reasons to keep this in mind. On a hot July day, snuggling with a vampire can be more refreshing than a cold lemonade. On the other hand, in the dead of winter, it's best to let him bite you before you get cozy.

Q: Did Jesse hypnotize those animals? Because in the movies, it seems you can always rely on dogs to resist the mind control of evil beings and tip off the good guys.

A: Don't count on your dog to tell it to you straight when a vampire is working his swirly eyes. Immortals can paralyze a Pomeranian or mesmerize a malamute as easily as they can enchant you.

Q: Can vampires recognize you by the scent of your blood? And do some people's blood smell more attractive to them?

A: I asked Colin these questions once. He told me that vampires indeed have an enhanced sense of smell and therefore many are connoisseurs of scent. There are subtle differences between one person's blood and another's, but it is really the scent of the whole person that vampires appreciate and admire. They do like the smell of blood, and it can whet their appetite just like the aroma of movie popcorn does for mortals; but vampires are driven by more than just the smell of their food, even as mortals are. Many of them seem to like honeysuckle, by the way. And, of course, pumpkin spice latte.

chapter 6

Your Guy Is a Vampire:
Some Practical Considerations

You've found yourself a vampire, wooed and won him; the temptation now is to sit back and enjoy your reward. But if you take that sort of *laissez-faire* position, I'm afraid you may be in for a rude awakening from your swirly-eyes-induced trance. There's more to dating a vampire than sleeping during the day and keeping a crucifix in the drawer.

YOUR RELIGIOUS DIFFERENCES

Of course we've already dismissed that after-dark-only issue; but since I brought it up, what about religion? Should you hide your crosses and not invite him to midnight mass at Christmas? What about Yom Kippur or a Star of David? Will your Buddha statue freak him out?

Not to worry, vampires actually come in all varieties of religions and will probably accept yours just fine. That aversion-to-sacred-objects business is just more old propaganda from the buzzkills who wanted everyone to think vampires are damned. Actually, according to Colin, part of the blame falls on vampire society itself. In days of yore there were not many ways to get press. Remember, we're not just talking pre-Internet — this was pre-Gutenberg. Your only alternatives were low-tech media like minstrels and stories around the campfire. As far as mass media, your best option was the Church. Unfortunately, the vampire message of bite-and-let-live was, shall we say, a bit too nuanced to communicate properly from the pulpit. So vampires, believing there's no such thing as bad press, opted to accept big bad headlines and put up with the consequences, kind of like happens with today's celebrities and the tabloids. At least it kept them in the news.

DO YOUR IMPERFECTIONS BUG HIM?

Trust me, the fact that you're a Baptist and he's a Lutheran will not be your biggest challenge. For one thing, it won't be easy coping with that dang perfection of his. We've already considered the upside of dating a perfect being, and don't get me wrong, it's nice. But the downside is that a vampire can give a girl a real inferiority complex.

This may hit you the first time you have seasonal allergies and your sneezing is ruining a romantic evening. "Guillaume never gets colds or flu," you'll lament to yourself. "It must be a pain for him to put up with my ailments." Or maybe you're sharing a bonfire and he's all about dancing in the flames. Of course, you know can't join him.

Meanwhile, it's all very well to be blown away by a guy's talents, but sometimes you want to be able to impress him in return. And how do you impress a vampire? You have to try to excel at things that he hasn't gotten around to trying yet, like, say, quilting. Of course, give him a sewing machine and a pile of fat quarters and he'll figure out how to make the most complicated Improved Nine Patch imaginable before suppertime.

In short, if one-upmanship is the game, you're fighting a losing battle.

Fortunately, with vampires the game may be pool, or whist, but it's *never* one-upmanship. Your immortal knew going in that you aren't perfect, and he likes you that way. In fact, he prefers it. After all, vampires get more than enough exposure to perfection by hanging around with each other. They're actually pretty starved for things like clumsiness and ineptitude. Vampires find that stuff quite endearing. So don't set impossible standards for yourself, just let you be you. Remember that it's your unique life force, your special vitality that drew him to you, and nothing can rob you of that.

NO WORK AND ALL SWOON

Alongside fending off feelings of inferiority, your other main challenge will be to keep your head a reasonable percentage of the time. Because I'm not going to lie, being in the presence of a vampire makes one tend to swoon and drift out of touch with daily life. And a person can't be swooning 24/7— it's just not practical.

It will take awhile to get the hang of this. On the one hand, you'll be conducting your regular activities of going to class or work, buying groceries, getting your transmission flushed and your computer defragged, etc. On the other hand, you'll be conversing about the

Spanish Inquisition, flying, nurturing another creature with your lifeblood, and being transported to transcendent realms beyond the senses. Believe me, you're in for a whole new kind of multi-tasking.

The temptation is to give yourself over to your vampire entirely, to let his beauty and power overwhelm you, so that you can forget about things like 1040 tax forms and what goes into which recycle bin. Giving in to that temptation is a mistake, for reasons that may not even occur to you.

The obvious reason is that your regular life cannot be ignored. The IRS will fine you for back taxes, your car will burn up its tranny, and you can't give up your job because you are, as previously discussed, not immune to ailments and need the health insurance.

The less obvious reason is that you really can burn out on swooning.

Overswooning, much like familiarity, breeds contempt. I'm not sure why that is, but it's true. You can prove it to yourself with a little experiment. Spend a day *not* thinking about your vampire. Put him utterly out of your mind, focus on the work piling up on your desk. Meanwhile, instead of daydreaming about his bite, think about your upcoming trip to visit your cousins in Cleveland.

The next time he pounces on you without warning and fixes you with his piercing stare, the thrill will be all new and fresh.

Overswooning, on the other hand, eventually robs your vampire of his appeal. If you focus continually on surrendering to him the law of diminishing returns will kick in and your vampire will quickly lose his appeal. He can still knock you out, no question, but you may find that after fixating all day on the bliss of capitulation, the actual experience seems a bit disappointing. What a shame!

WHEN YOUR PERFECT VAMPIRE FAILS YOU

And speaking of disappointment, believe it or not, a vampire *can* disappoint you. He may be everything you want him to be. (He can *control* your mind, not *read* it, dear.) He may be a little more fierce than you need after a hard day at the office, or not fierce enough when you are ready for nasty.

And seeing as you thought all this time he was perfect, brilliant, splendid, godlike, this sudden disappointment may be quite crushing. Much of the initial thrill of being with a vampire is due to your conviction that he is the ideal mate for you. That doesn't give a guy a lot of wiggle room.

So this is why in the early stages I recommend you try to remain lighthearted about your vampire relationship. Now I admit, being "lighthearted" about sharing your blood with an undead creature who may or may not be nasty might seem counterintuitive. But my point is this: your vampire affair is meant for fun. Never turn it into a project, an obsession, a puzzle, or worst of all, a problem. If the relationship is getting you down for some reason, just step back and look at yourself and laugh. You're dating a vampire! What about that says, "I should feel bummed"?

MAKE NEW FRIENDS, BUT KEEP THE OLD

Now, we've been talking all this while about the pair of you as if you are seeing each other exclusively. However, the odds are good that you are also dating a mortal. Many a woman already in a fulfilled, happy relationship meets a vampire and finds him just too cool to pass up (especially if he's entranced her into that conviction — then really, what can you do?). I personally think it's all kinds of healthy to date mortals and vampires at the same time, and my saying that shouldn't surprise you.

We just discussed the importance of avoiding overswooning. Your mortal boyfriend can keep your head from permanently disappearing into the clouds. He's most certainly going to distract you from thinking about your vampire all the livelong day. And the experiences you enjoy with your mortal boyfriend are meaningful and enjoyable in ways you can't quite derive from your blood-drinker. For one thing, it can be satisfying watching your boyfriend make his way through life successfully without being perfect. For another, he can help you with your taxes, and believe me, that's one thing no vampire's ever going to do for you.

On the flip side, there's the fact that hanging with the undead can help you be a better, stronger, more imaginative, more balanced person. It will surprise you how much better you can deal with your boyfriend's foibles, and also be a better girlfriend to him. But more on this in a later chapter.

My point is summed up in the verse from Ecclesiastes: "To everything there is a season, and a time to every purpose under heaven." Let your mortal boyfriend and your vampire each play his unique and important part in your life, and everyone wins!

i picked an undead loser

Sometimes your vampire boyfriend can truly let you down,
I'll admit. But when that happens, don't despair — there
are plenty of killer fish in the sea, as my friend Jen can attest.

*Well, calling Ludwig a "loser" is an exaggeration, but he was
just such a disappointment.*

*At first we got off to a great start. Ludwig was way more
exciting than my mortal boyfriend. I mean, he didn't work in
a carwash, and he was a much better dresser. I'm kind of Goth
myself, so I was sure having a vampire boyfriend was going to
totally rock.*

*But it turned out he was one of those really polite vampires.
I guess he just fell back on the overblown manners he was raised
with back in the 18th century. That's all nice, I guess, but I
wanted a lot more leering, and springing out at me from the
shadows, and "I want your blood." Can you believe he never
once towered over me and demanded, "I want your blood"?
I'm not saying he didn't have a predatory nature like a vampire
should, he just always tried to keep it in check. Bogus. It was
honestly making me depressed. And not in a good emo way
either. I mean, here I'd hooked up with an actual vampire and
he was so darn congenial. Sure, I could break up with him,
but what girl wants to throw away the chance to be with a
vampire?*

*Well, one day Ludwig sat me down (not as authoritatively
as I wanted, of course) and said he could tell I was unhappy.
He recommended (much too sweetly) that I consider dating his
friend, a vampire named Boris. I was glad for a way to gracefully bow out of seeing Ludwig, so I agreed.*

And Boris — well, let me tell you, Boris is a real *vampire.
I'd better not even go into the details. Wow.*

*And to be fair, I have to give props to Ludwig, too. He wasn't
much of a vampire, but at least he was, well, pretty wise.*

Case Study 106:

Me, Aidan, and the urge to give up mortals.

Aidan was born in Ireland in the 8th century, and is the oldest vampire I've ever met. In my experience, the older the vampire, the more eccentric he seems to be. I think that's because having lived through so many different times and cultures, old vampires simply can't quite fit in today's world. There are too many things they've done, too much they know that just doesn't jive with the limited experience of we recently-born mortals.

Aidan's eccentricity does not in any way limit his charm. He has a druidic sensibility, a strange but appealing appreciation for nature and its connection to the spiritual world. To put it another way, he can tap in to what modern people call magic and superstition. I can't deny it's a little scary at times, but all vampires are . . . that's why we love them.

Aidan invited me to go on a picnic with him once. Please set aside all your preconceived notions of a "picnic"; this was more like a one-day international trip. I can't tell you how he transported us to this place, which was so remote and deserted it looked like northwestern Ontario. It was a heavily forested spot on the shore of a pristine lake, and quietly, majestically beautiful.

Aidan found me a nice rock to sit on and admire the view. Meanwhile he disappeared into the forest, returning after twenty minutes with an immense dead tree trunk that would have required a troop of mortal men to carry. My vampire declared we couldn't have a proper picnic without a "faerie bench." He invited me to sit on the grass, and from our picnic basket amazingly produced a very sharp-looking axe. He split the wood, notched it, assembled it, and lashed it together to make a sort of wooden love seat. Aidan completed the project by pulling out his pocket knife and carving an insignia into the center of the back of the bench; it was a lovely Gaelic design that I didn't recognize.

"That, my darlin', is what makes it a faerie bench," Aidan told me, his hazel eyes twinkling in the afternoon sun.

He took his fishing pole — which also had fit in the picnic basket — down to the lake, to cast for trout. Meanwhile, I built a little fire pit and started a fire. It seemed we had also brought butter, potatoes, and onions with us, and by the time the sun was sinking behind the trees, we had a meal sizzling in our cast-iron frying pan. We sat on the faerie bench and ate it from tin plates.

When we were done and cleaned up, we sat back down on the bench, which was ridiculously and preternaturally comfortable for something hewn from a dead tree. I was anticipating some campfire storytelling from Aidan, for he was a true Irishman in that regard and there's not much I love more than vampire storytelling.

"So, darlin'," he said, "shall I show you some faeries, then?"

"Yes, please!" I replied, certainly not taking him literally.

He took my hand in his, which was nicely warmed by the fire. He lifted it to his lips, and then sunk his teeth into my wrist. I admit I was startled — a sudden bite is always a little flinch-worthy; but it wasn't shocking. After all, I was used to being in the company of vampires. Then I turned to gaze into the fire, and as Aidan fed, and the flames fluttered and danced, I saw the faeries arrive.

They came out of the woods, little glowing things not more than four inches tall. And they were different colors, reminding me of Sleeping Beauty's three fairy godmothers in the Disney movie. Each was a gorgeous monochromatic creature of a unique color: aquamarine, magenta, amber, lilac. Each was a tiny person, with a perfect little face, slender limbs, and, of course, wings.

I watched the faerie show for a half an hour: the dancing and swooping, the laughing and singing . . . I even picked out my favorite faerie, the amber-colored one, who was male and very fetching in a tiny way. I swear he flirted with me.

Aidan finished drinking, and a few minutes after that, the faeries bid farewell. As I watched them go, I was seized with a terrible sadness and loss. Suddenly the thought of my ordinary life horrified me. In Aidan's world one could be transported instantly to the wilderness, fishing poles fit in picnic baskets, and there were faeries. In my world there was cable TV, the mall . . . oh, I couldn't think of it without wanting to cry.

Aidan, who was as sensitive as he was eccentric, said, "Oh, now, darlin', don't you be lookin' so forlorn! I can make you another faerie bench one day, you know."

"But my real life is so . . . dull and plain," I said. "And my mortal boyfriend is sweet, but, he's just nothing like you, Aidan."

"Ah, there you go makin' that mistake again, my girl," said Aidan. "Makin' too much of a difference between one part o' life and another. It's all one big, happy whole to my way o' thinkin'."

It didn't seem like one big, happy whole to me just then, but I tried to believe him, because very old vampires like Aidan generally know more than I do.

It was maybe a week later when I was out on a walk one night with my mortal boyfriend, Alan. Alan was studying astrological physics. As we walked, he was telling me about quasars with wide-eyed enthusiasm. I don't know what came over me, but I heard myself say, "Quasars are cool I'm sure, Alan, but they're not faeries."

"You believe in faeries?" he asked.

I didn't want to lie, but I also didn't want him to think I was a lunatic, so I hesitated.

"Because faeries are theoretically possible," he said. "There's plenty of room for faeries in what I know of quantum physics."

I stared at him, with my mouth open.

"I'm just saying," he said. "But I think they'd have to be monochromatic on an individual basis. Could be various colors, mind you — but each one would have to be various shades of the same hue."

I could hardly believe my ears. I stood there, stunned, for a minute.

Then I gave Alan a big kiss.

FAQS ABOUT THE UNDEAD

Q: So crucifixes and holy water don't work. What about stakes?
A: Your question, really, is can one kill a vampire? Or was Buffy bogus? As much as Joss Whedon did tend to emphasize the nasty vampires, far be it from me to criticize anyone so enamored of our undead friends. Yes, you can kill a vampire with a stake to the heart but that's for another book.

Q: How do vampires get around having to pay taxes?
A: Man, I get that question a lot. Okay, vampires don't need to be face-to-face, employing their hypnotic eyes, to perform mind control. They can do it over the phone, too.

IRS Agent: Mr. Vladimir, it's come to our attention that you haven't paid any taxes since, well, ever.
Mr. Vladimir: I am not the citizen you want to audit.
IRS Agent: Beg pardon, I just realized you're not the citizen I want to audit.

Q: So do most vampires like wearing black? How about capes? Eyeliner?
A: I dared to ask Mordred once about "vampiric affectations." (His black leather gloves, for example.) He told me that each immortal has his or her own sense of style, but as a society they do take note of mortal expectations and aim to please. They find it amusing to appear in the forms that most entrance us. Are some of the undead going for the sparkly-skin look? You'll have to be on the lookout . . .

Part Three:
Dr. Steven Grey/Conner's Letter of Warning

Conner holds a very special place in my heart. He has always taken it upon himself to be a sort of vampiric guardian angel to me, if such a thing is possible. One day, I let it slip that I found Steven Grey an "interesting and compelling character." Conner's response was immediate and forceful. So forceful, in fact, that he scared me out of my wits. I left his house at once, feeling ill and trembling all over. My departure is what inspired this letter of apology — and warning.

Dearest Diana,

It is never my wish to lose control of my behaviour, certainly not in the presence of a mortal, least of all you. Alas, I am a vampire and therefore in certain states of displeasure it is difficult for me to reign in my passions. I cannot blame you for your curiosity and your uninformed remarks, nor am I happy that they resulted in my violent reaction. Nevertheless, to put it plainly, Steven Grey is evil. I cannot possibly exaggerate that point.

I understand the appeal of this sort of fellow to many women. Certainly I know very well that fear, horror, and even disgust can be fascinating. In particular, I understand your own personal temptations to dally with the sinister. Nevertheless, this is no time to even daydream of yielding to such temptations.

Grey is a distinguished and charismatic man, and without doubt an expert at seduction — both psychological and supernatural. He employs those assets as a predator's tools. He will never use them for anything else, he has no other goal than to torture and torment your kind and mine. Meanwhile, his charms are such that nothing about his behaviour toward you will give you the slightest clue of his intentions.

To make matters worse, I fear your friendship with me might make you a target for this demon. I am the very sort of vampire to whom he takes greatest umbrage, utterly opposed as I am to his goals for our kind. In fact, he is the reason I choose to live in this part of the world: I consider it my mission to keep an eye on him and protect his potential victims whenever I can.

I cannot be sure that Grey would harm you, or even take any notice of you (particularly if you do not wear the ribbon, and I assume you would never do such a dangerous thing). However, when I think of the possibility of him having his, harming you as he has so many others, I am tempted into a fury far exceeding what I displayed last night.

I am not your master, much as I sense you would like me to be, nor do I require your obedience in exchange for my love. I will care for you regardless of your actions. However, Grey is crafty and skillful, and I am far from certain of any success when I oppose him. In the past I have indeed failed more than once.

I cannot bear to envision what misery an association with Grey could bring to you. This, then, is the reason why I gave in to rage at even the suggestion. I hope you understand now the reason for my outburst. And please, please, dear Diana — forget Grey and spare no effort in keeping yourself out of his path!
Affectionately, I remain,
Yours,
Conner

chapter 7

Vampire Lovers Unite! Dealing with Those Who Dis the Lifestyle

there have always been misbehaving vampires who have given a bad name to their kind, and down through the ages, even innocent, good vampires have been the victims of predjudice. Today, though they may not bear torches and pitchforks, some people are going to try to discourage you from pursuing a happy relationship with a vampire.

As in much of life, you'll find it easier to deal with this by changing yourself, your attitude, and your approach, rather than putting energy into trying to change the minds of your critics. That said, I assure you that there are ways of coping other than giving in to those who would keep you and your immortal boyfriend apart. I've fended off all kinds of criticism over the years, so I hope you can benefit from my experience. So before you start feeling like some graveyard version of Romeo and Juliet, read on.

AVPS AND ADPS

Obviously, not everyone appreciates vampire dating. Let's divide and conquer by looking at the two main categories of your opponents: (1) those who oppose the vampire part, and (2) those who oppose the dating part. You see, some people honestly get vampires, but wouldn't be caught dead dating one . . . while others don't buy into immortals in the first place.

We'll take the latter group first. The Anti-Vampire People (AVP) simply don't understand why anyone is into the undead. They find vampires creepy and scary, which they can be, of course. The problem is they think your fascination with blood-drinkers is weird and inexplicable. They have all kinds of disagreeable misconceptions about what makes immortals attractive to their fans.

On the other hand, the Anti-Dating People (ADP) can see the appeal of vampires, all right . . . but they consider them strictly imaginary amusements, fitting for the movies and books but not relevant to one's daily life.

Certainly you can elect to ignore these people, wear your red satin ribbon with pride, and simply go ahead with your lifestyle choice. But if we're talking about someone important in your life — your family, your best friend, your mortal boyfriend — the issue will need to be addressed. You're probably going to have to help your loved ones understand why you're seeing a vampire, and find ways to convince them to put their farm tools away before they arrange an intervention or something.

It helps to keep in mind that, truthfully, your relatives and friends are not so much concerned about the vampire as they are about you.

They're wondering if this "obsession" of yours will cause you to do something crazy and self-destructive, like moving to Romania or getting your lips pierced. Does it mean you have a death wish? Will you dye all your clothes black and wear a cape? Will you stop hanging around with regular mortals, bleach your skin, rob blood banks?

DON'T BE COLD — HELP THEM CHILL

Before these people panic themselves into a frenzy, you need to reassure them. That reassurance should address the following three topics:

1. What it is that you like about vampires. There's a lot to like, but try to choose those aspects that appeal to the naysayers before you. Find common ground or focus on their concerns. For example, family members will like to hear this sort of thing: "The idea of eternal fidelity to one's true love appeals to me and vampires represent that faithfulness and devotion." Best girlfriends need to hear things like: "Well, you know, real guys can't be perfect . . . but vampires can, and that's pretty refreshing." Boyfriends might enjoy hearing: "You're such a super nice guy — spending time with vampires gets the 'bad boy' out of my system so I can better appreciate how wonderful you are."

2. How your life is improved by vampires. The pessimists worry that your "interest" is harmful and will inhibit you from living real life to the full. You need to help them see that, on the contrary, your mental health actually benefits from the association. Say things like: "Thinking about my interest in vampires has

taught me some helpful things about myself." Like what? "Well, like I'm working on finding a good balance between giving in to what people want from me, and standing up for myself."

3. The fact that you haven't lost perspective. Whether it's vampires or some more commonplace hobby like scrapbooking, people are put off when they think someone might be obsessed. Sometimes all it takes to calm down the worrywarts is demonstrating that you have both a sense of balance and a sense of humor about your vampire avocation. "Sure, I think a vampire could be an ideal boyfriend," you say, laughing. "They're attractive, experienced, mysterious, and can't beg off taking you out because they feel crappy or are broke. What's not to like?"

EMBRACE YOUR OWN VAMPIROPHILIA

The best way to cope with anti-vampire criticism is to be secure in yourself. Sadly, however, our culture doesn't exactly teach us to embrace and cherish our love of the undead. It's easy to fall prey to self-doubt. Sometimes you ask yourself, "Why am I dating a vampire? Who dates vampires, anyway?" If you've been spending a lot of time with him, or constantly thinking about him, you may yourself wonder if you're obsessed. That's a surefire way to creep yourself out — and if *you're* creeped out about your vampire relationship, you can't expect others to accept it.

how to come out as the mate of a vampire

Everyone's situation is different, so I'm not about to dictate exactly how you should handle your own "coming out." But here are some general suggestions that I've found helpful.

Who should you tell? *Anyone who will be receptive.*

You can use the support of those who appreciate the appeal of vampires. On the flip side, if you expect a bad reception to the news, there's nothing wrong with keeping your love life private, just as is true for people in relationships with other controversial types, like lawyers and politicians.

How should you explain? *Well, start with a preemptive strike against objections, like, "I assure you I have no intention of becoming one myself, but . . ." If your listener's potential concerns are already alleviated, he or she will deal much better with the "I'm dating this really wonderful vampire" part. And be sure to have answers prepared in advance for those questions you expect, like "Oh my god, do you let him drink your blood?!?" That way you can give calm replies like, "Why, yes — but safely, of course."*

How can you get others to take the relationship seriously? *Some people will think this is just a phase, like when you wanted to become a rock star but quit guitar lessons after two weeks. You can't force others to see your genuine commitment to your vampire, and getting that tattoo of "I ♥ Aurelius" on your ankle won't get it done. Only time will demonstrate your faithful devotion to the undead, so have patience.*

How should you deal with objections from your vampire boyfriend's people? *In any relationship, both parties have friends and families who may object. What if your vampire's best friend thinks he should get back together with his last girlfriend? What if his Maker doesn't approve of you? Well, fortunately you don't have to worry about such matters yourself. Vampires have their own ways of "persuading" their own kind, and trust me, Aurelius will make sure you are accepted with open arms.*

SECRETS . . . AND CELEBRATIONS!

So, how can you be a true vampire fan without bringing criticism down on your head? Well, first of all, it never hurts to have a secret life. In fact, having a secret life can be tons of fun, just ask any vampire. Or any mortal for that matter: I'll bet a lot of amateur golfers like to pretend they're Tiger Woods once in awhile. Just because there are activities you prefer to keep on the down low, doesn't mean there's anything wrong with them.

Speaking of secrets, here's one: People who have rich inward lives have rich outward ones, too. I'm testimony to that. I've spent half my life hanging out in fantastical places with fantastical people. And I'm not the only one.

FIND FELLOW FANG FANCIERS

I also highly recommend you find some other vampire fans with whom to commune. Chances are they will be people who have given the matter quite a bit of thought and appreciate immortals for reasons similar to yours. Consequently, they will help you feel less defensive and more secure in your vampirophilia, and you can do the same for them.

Certainly the Internet offers some good and helpful communities for vampire lovers. Of course, you do want to be careful and selective about connections made over the Web. Real vampires never make arrangements to meet with mortals online; they think that's the ultimate in tacky. But feel free to share thoughts and ideas on the Web with other vampire fans . . . you might even make some new and excellent mortal friends that way.

Meanwhile, don't forget to seek out like-minded people among your own acquaintance. Bring up the subject of favorite vampires at a party and you may be amazed how many people you know possess some affection for the undead! And look for red-satin-ribbon wearers wherever you go. Vampire dating may not be for everyone, but I daresay the majority of people feel at least some curiosity, if not actual admiration, for these beings that you and I love so well.

Case Study 107:

Dan, Gwendolyn, and the AVP.

My name is Dan, and I'm a photographer. My specialty is "urban exploration" photography — I like to sneak into abandoned buildings late at night, set up interesting lighting, and take pictures that are admittedly somewhat bizarre. I suppose with a nocturnal hobby like that, I was bound to run into a vampire eventually.

One night I found this amazing old church, very baroque, and spent hours setting up the lighting. I used a lot of reds, very beautiful but ominous. So, a little after midnight, I started taking the photos. I happened to look back through the first dozen on the LCD and spotted what looked like a female figure peeking out from an archway. "What's this?" I said out loud.

"That's me," said a velvet voice behind me.

I whirled around, my heart in my throat, to find a woman standing right behind me. She had gorgeous dark eyes, and dark red hair, and she was so beautiful I thought I was hallucinating. I was terrified. As gorgeous as this woman was, there was a danger radiating off her. A lioness is beautiful too, but you don't want to get too close to one — and I felt she was too close to me, much too close.

She gave me a smile that went through me like a shiver, and said, "Can I help?"

I had this sudden, intense craving to let this woman bite me on the neck, and then I knew what I was dealing with: a vampire. I fought back the suicidal urge and backed up, away from her and from my camera on its tripod. Dared I try to make a run for it? I honestly feared for my life, even though the vampire hadn't done anything specifically threatening.

"I'm Gwendolyn," she said pleasantly, and then cast her eyes away from my face and onto my camera. "It's late for a mortal to be taking pictures. But these aren't typical pictures, I'm sure. Can I look at what you have so far?"

I nodded, speechless, and then realized I was going to have to approach her to show her the photos on the camera's LCD. She leaned close to the screen as I operated the buttons. My fingers were so close to her perfect face, I could feel coolness coming off her skin. Desire rose in me as I battled with my fear; Gwendolyn was the loveliest woman I'd ever seen, and I photograph professional models all the time. She wasn't just pretty . . . she was magical.

"What's your name?" she asked me as she looked at my shots.

"Dan," I replied.

"Dan, these are beautiful."

With those words I felt my fear diminish. Gwendolyn still seemed dangerous, but I had a sudden conviction that she didn't want to hurt *me*. So we sat down in one of the dusty pews and talked. She told me that she was born on a sheep farm in Wales almost 300 years ago. As the conversation went on, I marveled at how amazing she was. Gwendolyn was certainly a modern woman (she had an iPod in her jeans pocket), but had so much broader an understanding of the world and humanity and the meaning of existence than anyone I'd ever met.

The encounter was surreal. I never forgot for a moment that she was undead and immortal. Meanwhile, I concluded the meeting as if it were utterly mundane, by giving her a ride home and asking for her phone number.

Gwendolyn and I dated for the next few months. Without doubt, I was in love with her. I wanted desperately to have her be part of everything in my life, but something told me not to be hasty about that. My gut feeling, as it turned out, was right. Even though I tried to keep it a secret that I was seeing a vampire, my friends somehow learned the truth.

One of my oldest friends, Carmen, had asked me to photograph her wedding. Then suddenly, a month before the day, she called me and said she'd worked out other plans. I was confused at first, and then Carmen told me, "Dan, I got your RSVP and saw it was for two; I assume you were planning on bringing that new girlfriend of yours."

My decision to do that hadn't been easy, but I was persistent. "Yes, I'm bringing Gwen," I said.

There was a long pause. Then Carmen said, "I'm sorry, Dan — but I hope you can understand why I wouldn't want her there. I mean, what she is and all. It's my *wedding*, Dan."

The unfairness of this hit me like a wall. I thought of Gwendolyn, and how wise and self-assured and brilliant she was, and how if Carmen only knew her, she would be ashamed. At the same time I remembered my own fear that first night in the old church. Gwen was not ordinary in any way, and as wonderful as that was, it would always be an obstacle.

My silence had gone on longer than I realized. I was awakened from these reveries by Carmen's voice on the phone. "Dan, are you there?" she asked. I could hear in her voice then that she knew she'd hurt me, and was on some level sorry for that.

"I'm here," I said. "It's a shame you feel that way. But I can't come without her. I'm sorry."

"Me, too."

"You'd like Gwendolyn, Carmen. You should meet her."

"Maybe another time," she said.

But not as if she meant it.

FAQS ABOUT THE UNDEAD

Q: Is it really so easy to tell if someone's a vampire?

A: Certainly no one ever makes the mistake of taking a vampire for a plain old mortal. They come across immediately as special, and most people also pick up on the supernatural allure and their own sudden urge to be bitten. Putting two and two together, therefore, is not hard. Unless you're the kind of person who goes around wanting to be bitten by random people, meeting a vampire will seem out of the norm, to say the least.

Q: So you can really take a photograph of a vampire?

A: Yes. Photographing a vampire works just fine with today's digital cameras. But believe me, it was a problem in the old days with film cameras, something to do with silver being part of the technology.

Q: You said vampires can't see themselves in mirrors though . . . is that right?

A: It's true, they can't. It's that silver problem again, because the back of a mirror is silvered. On the other hand, a vampire can see himself in a webcam. That's why so many vampires have webcam-equipped laptops in their bathrooms. Thanks to modern technology, they can finally check if their hair looks okay. Which of course it always does.

chapter 8

Pitfalls to a Life of Satisfying Vampire Romance

most people who choose to pursue a life incorporating their love of vampires do so recognizing that there will be challenges, and we've discussed a lot of those challenges already. However, if you're like I was when I started out, there are a couple of areas of difficulty you've failed to consider.

One is the vampire himself. The other is you.

VAMPIRE ROMANCE THAT DOESN'T END HAPPILY EVER AFTER? WHA?

"The vampire himself"? you're asking. "I have no problem with that — I *love* vampires!" But I'm not talking about vampiric aspects in general — I'm talking about *your* vampire's specific personality

quirks . . . his habits, his values, his goals. Sure, you adore his penetrating gaze and the way he employs the twist-of-the-wrist power gesture. But how about his propensity for the blood of petite redheads? That's not quite so delightful every day of the week, is it?

Vampires are no different than people, and a relationship with one brings the same trials and tribulations. In fact, the challenge is exacerbated by the typical vampire's aversion to monogamy. You have your desires, he has his, and sometimes you will not be on the same page. You may think this won't matter, seeing as *his* page is beautiful old parchment penned in Gothic handwriting and you think you'll love it no matter what . . . but it *will* matter, trust me.

And even if your page is Office Max copier paper with plain old black Helvetica type, it still matters to you. There will be days when you'd really like him to look at your mundane little page and pay attention. There will be days, believe it or not, when you're tired of focusing on his lovely parchment and its flouncy calligraphy. Yes. There will be days ahead when he stops being one-hundred-percent desirable.

Well, this seems like a real bummer. Did I really bring you this far on the journey, tantalizing you with my tales of sexy, wonderful vampires, just to arrive at this juncture? Just to tell you that your vampire relationship will end up like any number of mortal relationships you've gone through and tried to forget by reading vampire romance books?

Not to worry. I'm a realist, but I still believe in love, and I promise all will come round in the end.

By staring bravely now into the potential pitfalls, you can prepare yourself to minimize and avoid them in the future. It takes wisdom and determination, but if you heed my advice you'll be able to maximize the fun of your vampire love affairs and minimize the angst.

And I suspect you already know a little bit about the angst. Angst-minimization sounds good, doesn't it? Okay then, let's start our little Tour of Pitfalls.

TOO MUCH TIME IN HIS LAIR

I previously brought up the issue of overswooning. Now let's look at this problem in a more comprehensive way. Just as a vampire can charm you into becoming his consort in the first place, his fantastical lifestyle can overwhelm you. When you first met him, all you could think about was the when and where of that first bite, the moment you would know for sure that you were, in some sense you could only imagine, together. But after that deal is done, you find out just how much more there is to being with a vampire. And it's all mighty seductive.

For one thing, your vampire boyfriend is definitely going to live in cooler digs than you. The "lairs" of modern vampires are typically spectacular: waterfront condos, restored Victorian mansions, 4,000 square-foot treehouses in the Amazon jungle, that sort of thing. I don't care if your own house has stainless-steel appliances, hardwood floors, a home theater and a spa tub; your vampire's place will be better.

Naturally, you will want to spend as much time as possible in his lair. Who wouldn't, not even taking into account that your host is Adonis-like? Why would you want to hang out anywhere else?

Nevertheless, it is possible to spend too much time in a vampire's lair, which of course I am using as a metaphor for being generally preoccupied with him and his world. You're probably expecting that now I will launch into a lecture about neglecting your responsibilities, losing touch with your friends, but I won't. You're a smart cookie, you've got plenty of sense. . . . I'm perfectly confident you will continue to be a good citizen even while hanging with the undead.

The problem is not the effect it will have on those around you — it's the effect it will have on *you*. Just like with overswooning, too much lair can kill the thrill. If you find suddenly the idea of playing hide-and-feed in his private labyrinth has lost its appeal, it's time to take a break. You need some You Time, whether that be a girls' weekend at the Mall of America, taking a pottery class, or reading some of your romance fiction books that don't include vampires. After your fangless vacation, you'll be refreshed and ready for vampiric delights once again.

On the flip side, too much lair can impart self-doubt, the fear that your vampire is too hard to hang onto. Focusing on his life rather than yours may make you feel he's so wonderful, you're so ordinary, his world is so amazing and unattainable, yours is so mundane, and so forth. When you feel like this it can help to draw back a bit from lair living, just to reconnect with what it is about you and your life that is cool, interesting, and worth enjoying.

Even if you really aren't inclined to take a break from the lair, I recommend you do, especially if you are hearing a tiny voice in the back of your head suggesting it. After all, it can't hurt. It's not like your vampire is going anywhere; even if he is, he can be back in the blink of an eye.

DON'T LET THE SWIRLY-EYED ONE PUSH YOU AROUND

Sometimes, however, the problem is not you, it's your vampire. Given that he can make you do whatever he wants, even the most upstanding vampire can accidentally find himself taking advantage. I've made the point that an immortal's power over you is a large part of his appeal — that Inner Mina business — but things can go too far and result in the unpleasant total loss of your autonomy.

So even if you feel like catering to your vampire's every whim, you may in fact, on some level, really wish you could turn him down occasionally (for specific tips, see "How to Say No to a Vampire," page 81). It's not that most vampires make unpleasant requests — they're actually pretty good about that for the most part — but sometimes they can get carried away with the "give yourself over to me" and the "come away with me into the night at once" and the "bring me over some fresh-baked oatmeal cookies."

Think about it: how healthy can a relationship be when "no" is simply not an option for you? I know I said that letting out your Inner Mina can be fun and helpful, but that doesn't mean you want to become a total zombie. Vampires = cool. Zombies = not cool. So what should you do to subtly and safely suggest to your immortal that he back off a bit with the commands?

Actually, the answer is pretty simple. Just like in mortal relationships, you need to communicate and compromise. Like this sort of exchange:

Vampire: I command you, make another batch of oatmeal cookies!

Mortal: Master, with all due respect and I'm not complaining, but I've been doing a lot of baking lately. I'm starting to feel like you're just in this for the cookies.

Vampire: Your cookies are good.

Mortal: But this is the third batch this week. I need a break, my lord.

Vampire: Sorry, I'd lost count. I command you to take a break from baking, until next month!

Mortal: Thank you, master.

Will he be upset by your assertiveness? Of course not. Remember, I told you vampires love swoony women with spunk.

I CAN'T BELIEVE IT — MY VAMPIRE BETRAYED ME

I don't know why it catches us off guard, considering his perfect looks and mind control skills, but few are prepared for our vampire to cheat on us. Shouldn't we have suspected this, after seeing all those movie vampires with their little troupes of fanged female groupies waiting in the wings? But I suppose we forget because typically our vampires seem so completely entranced and utterly devoted to us.

It's certainly true that vampire love is intense — they are so adept at finding things to love about each one of us. But I'm not gonna lie, as a culture the undead do tend to stray. Sure, there are one-woman guys among them. Keep in mind, though, it's hard enough for a man with a 75-year life span to be faithful to one woman. I think even you or I would be ready for a change after a few centuries.

. . . *follow me to page 122*

is he cheating and why?

I realized the title of my story sounds like a punchline from a lawyer joke: "Izzy, Cheating & Why, Attys. at Law." That's okay, now you know I have a sense of humor about my vampire problems.

I'm Serena, and I'm not the kind of vampire-lover who goes for intimidating, pushy immortals. I was drawn to Sylvestri because he was the strong, silent type. I love that in a vampire.

We had an amazing relationship for months. But then, one day, Sylvestri started to change. He lost his sexy inscrutability. He became chatty, yammering on to me about celebrity gossip and such. My vampire's personality turned into something completely unattractive!

You might think it silly, but another thing that bothered me was his text messages. Sylvestri always had the most amazing way of texting. He was so fast with the buttons he could write long romantic tomes to me on his iPhone. Then one day things changed. Suddenly it was "CALL U L8R" and "NOT 2NITE SRY." Completely out of character.

And then one night I got this text from him: "MET SOME1 NEW, …HAVE 2 BR8K UP W/U." Can you believe that? He broke up with me by text! I would have been a lot more upset were it not for the fact that Sylvestri had become so lame. It wasn't going to be that hard to get over him.

Then I remembered a conversation I'd had with him a few months before. I told him how I had this new job, and this new mortal boyfriend, and I felt like with all that and a vampire too, I was spread too thin. I suddenly realized Sylvestri had intentionally made himself unappealing to me.

Now I'm convinced he actually did me a favor. In a pretty inscrutable way, I'll grant you, but it ended up being okay.

Okay, now I bet some of you are rather irritated with me. I say I believe in vampire love and now this? Before you strip me of my red satin ribbon, hear me out. I actually don't view this news as crushing; in fact I find it rather liberating. Let me explain.

There's a definite place for fidelity, monogamy, and life-long commitment. And when it comes to your mortal relationships, these are musts. In the realm of vampires, however, I find things play a bit differently. But you know what? That goes both ways. Today you are convinced you could never love anyone but this particular immortal, but next month, if a new vampire comes along, wouldn't it be nice to get to know him as well?

Well, that's exactly how vampires feel, and fortunately they have plenty of love and attention to go around. I've found most of them quite remarkable in that way. They are crazy about you until the petite redhead shows up . . . and then they are crazy about her BUT they're still crazy about you, too! Vampires don't lose interest in one victim when they find another . . . that's the wonderful thing about them.

So now does that troupe-of-females thing make more sense? Don't think of it in a negative way, like some kind of harem. (Old horror movies always tend to spin the vampire lifestyle in a downbeat way.) No, think of it more like accumulating friends.

Even when a vampire throws you over, it's not necessarily a time to despair. Serena's story confirms that you needn't despair if your vampire takes up with someone else. Think of it as your own pass to have more than one vampire in your life as well. The vampire world is not a place where you have to put restrictions on adventure.

That's why I like it so much.

Me, Conner, and a lesson in "vampire infidelity."

It happened to me with Conner: the "cheating."

Conner was a young mortal, and a young vampire in Britain in the 14th century. He got to be around when Chaucer's *Canterbury Tales* was a hit, and Malory popularized the story of King Arthur, and, of course, when the Bard himself was making history. In those days no one had yet dared to put on paper the dark rumors about blood-drinkers that were just starting to circulate in Europe and the British Isles. Before his conversion, Conner actually considered doing so himself, for he was an aspiring writer and well known for his storytelling in that corner of Britain. However, once he was converted he thought better of the idea.

Conner, as you know, is a very special vampire to me, and already had become such at the time of this anecdote. Conner would be very much my type even if he were mortal. He has long, wavy black hair, and deep brown eyes, and a largish nose — something I've always found very attractive. He is lanky of limb, and somehow manages to be simultaneously graceful and ungainly, a bit like the Scarecrow in *The Wizard of Oz* movie. That makes him sound merely cute, though, and he is hardly that. There is an immutable magnificence in everything about Conner.

Meanwhile, he is indeed a divine storyteller and you know how I like that. Conner's imagination is boundless. His way with the English language — Old, Middle, or modern — indeed rivals Shakespeare's. Conner has told me stories that made me laugh till I wept, and stories that scared me so much I was afraid to go to sleep, and stories that made me cry they were so grand and real and poignant.

The first time we spoke was at an outdoor festival, sitting at a picnic table listening to a band playing New Orleans jazz. I knew after five minutes that I was going to fall in love with him. In fact, after an hour of listening to and critiquing trumpet music, and ways to prepare shrimp, and the works of Anne Rice, I wondered if I'd ever be able to love anyone else but Conner.

I wanted very badly for Conner to drink from me that first evening, but he is the sort to take his time about important things and begged off, offering me a kiss instead. The kiss was quite sufficient to make me want to turn over my soul to him forever. His hair in my fingers was so soft, his mouth was so gentle and promised so much. His arms around me were frightening and soothing all at once. It was so hard to part from him; it hurt physically.

Fortunately, after that we met nearly every night at his lair. Conner had a fire pit in his backyard, with a big two-person hammock set up so he can hold you close, be near the fire, and tell you tales.

I was head over heels about Conner and felt it was impossible for a mortal to be happier than I was. But underneath that raging elation, I was also worried.

There was something untamable about Conner, something I couldn't put my finger on. Oh, of course, all vampires are untamable, but it was harder to understand it in one so well-mannered and pleasant as Conner. Still, some of the stories he told me were so strange and frightening — like the one about the sky eating itself — that I was always mindful of his wildness. It wasn't that I worried he would be unfaithful to me, exactly. It was just that I also felt much, much too small to be his whole world, like he was mine.

And soon I found out that, indeed, I wasn't his whole world.

One night we had no plans to meet, but I missed him so much I went to his house to see if he might be at home. No one answered my knock and the house was dark, so I went around back to see if he might be at the fire pit.

I rounded the corner of the house, and froze in my tracks. Indeed, there were two people in the hammock, and I heard Conner's beautiful voice speaking . . . telling a story to someone else. I was too horrified to move. Why I stood there I don't know. Then I saw him bite her, and that was too much to bear.

When you're upset with a vampire, you can't get away with simply not answering his phone calls. If he asks you what's wrong, you can't tersely say, "nothing" and walk away – the silent treatment doesn't work. Vampires can find out the truth in short order, so none of that is any use.

Conner showed up at my house. I didn't want to talk to him. I was a little fearful of what he wanted with me. But I invited him in — his eyes insisted I tell him what was wrong.

"I can't believe you cheated on me," I said to him through my tears. "You not only told someone else a story; you drank from her!"

"How did I cheat on you, angel?" he asked. "It was a story I told you last week — and not even a particularly good one, I think."

Conner truly looked confused. Although obviously he was not grasping my objections, he seemed contrite simply because I was upset. After a moment of concentration, he said, "So it bothers you that you aren't the only one with whom I share myself."

"Yes," I said, sniffling.

He lifted his hand to stroke my hair. "But it takes nothing from you, don't you see?" he said. "As I said — it was a story I already told you. And I wouldn't be happy only telling it to her — I wouldn't be happy if I couldn't share it with *you*. You know I keep nothing from you, everything I am is yours. But if you can't bear it if others partake of me as well, then . . . well, I'm not sure what we are to do."

Although his words weren't especially comforting, I felt a little bit better. I think it was because of the way he looked at me, so intent and chagrined and worried. I felt better, but I knew we were still at a terrible impasse. "Conner," I said, putting my hand on his chest, "it's just that I want you to be mine. To belong to me."

A warm smile lit up his face. "Oh, is that all?" he asked. "Well, of course I do. That's easy."

I realized what he said did not, to Conner, contradict anything he had said before. To his mind, he indeed belonged utterly to me. It was simply that he belonged utterly to other people as well. I was not sure I could get my mind around that, and meanwhile I was very sure it didn't make me completely happy.

I guess he was able to read these emotions in my face. He brushed the tears off my cheek with his cool fingers. Then he said, "Diana . . . tell me if you belong completely to me."

"Of course."

"And tomorrow, if you meet another vampire, say, a tall, blond one, with broad shoulders and one of those scruffy short beards you women go so gaga for, and he sings like an angel and has a private plane and can make up poetry whenever he likes. In iambic pentameter, with internal rhymes and everything. Let's say he's too wonderful not to love. Will you still belong completely to me? Think carefully."

I stared into his dark, shining eyes, and I thought carefully. "Yes," I said.

"Even when you're drinking champagne on his plane while he makes rhymes for your name?"

"That was a poem, Conner."

"Yes I know, I did that intentionally . . . although it wasn't very good. Well?"

"Yes," I said, feeling myself smile. "Yes, I will still belong to you."

"Maybe to him and me at the same time, because with vampires, it can work that way," said Conner.

"Yes," I said, "I see it can." I thought a moment. Then I told him, "Perhaps you're not my whole world either, to be perfectly honest."

He grinned and kissed my forehead. "Now then," he told me with mock sternness, "you must come round my house tomorrow night, and see the logs I invented that burn in colors. I also have a new story, and I'd like you to hear it first."

"That would be lovely," I said.

FAQS ABOUT THE UNDEAD

Q: Can you elaborate on how vampires earn a living? How do they afford the expensive Liquid Shade and their fancy homes and sports cars and all that? It seems they always have the cool jobs.

A: There are cases of "regular Joe" vampires, who happily make their livings fixing up cars, doing construction, or serving as cops or firefighters. But yes, the majority are rock stars, models, actors, high-powered ad execs . . . yes, clearly vampires typically get the glamorous, high-paying jobs. But think about it, if three people are interviewing for a great position and one is a vampire, who do you think is going to get the job? That said, though, I want to make it clear that immortals do not cheat to get ahead, like hypnotizing their bosses into giving them raises and promotions and extra perks. A vampire really doesn't need to cheat, given that great skill set of his.

Q: Does every vampire have a sense of humor?

A: Nearly all the nice ones do, and actually, sense of humor is a good litmus test for telling bad vampires from evil ones. Bad vampires can be really menacing, aggressive, and domineering, but then they'll totally lighten the mood with a good pun or reference to the latest popular YouTube video. Evil vampires don't do funny. If you think an evil vampire might be doing a Bela Lugosi impression for you, trust me, it's not an impression — that happens to be his real voice.

Q: It sounds like monogamy is not a vampire's favorite lifestyle choice. Do they ever get married?

A: There are all kinds of vampires and yes, some do marry. (However, please don't draw your mental picture of that from *Bride of Dracula*.) Even though I spent this chapter making a case for a lighter, more frivolous view of vampire relationships, things indeed can get quite serious with vampires. There is, after all (wait for it), conversion. And I do believe it's time to talk about that in the next chapter.

Part Four:
Dr. Steven Grey/In His Clutches

I knew I needed to become less obsessed with Conner, to have other things going on in my life, so I stopped seeing him as much. It was time to get some balance, some perspective.

I had all the best intentions.

One day I happened to receive in the mail an adult education flyer from one of the local colleges. In paging through it, I discovered there was a six-week course on Tuesday nights called "Vampires in Literature." And who was to be guest instructor but Professor Steven Grey!

My heart raced. The idea was madness! But it was an adult ed course, I would be in a roomful of people on a college campus. How could that be dangerous? I could realize my dream of meeting Dr. Grey, and play it safe.

It would be a good distraction from Conner, I told myself. I'd get the whole thing out of my system once and for all, I told myself. It wasn't like Dr. Grey was a serial killer anymore, I told myself. . . .

I had to stop thinking about it before I changed my mind. I went online, and signed up.

The first night of class I was, of course, terribly nervous. I took a seat in the classroom about halfway back — my attempt at blending in. Sitting around me were twenty other students, a mixed bag of ages, about half women and half men. Promptly at 7:00 p.m., Dr. Grey made his entrance. He wore a charcoal-gray sport coat over his pearl-gray chambray shirt and jeans.

Just like In his photo online, he was painfully attractive. No one else in the room gave any sign of recognizing our professor as a vampire, not that I expected them to.

As he got the discussion underway, I paid very, very close attention to him. I suppose, to the unsuspecting, Dr. Grey seemed articulate, charming, brilliant . . . and unthreatening. At worst the others might see him as stern, with an acerbic wit. I, however, who had read his essay and heard about him from my vampire friends, could sense the carefully veiled menace. On the several occasions when his eyes connected with mine, I could plainly see an ominous gleam.

It sent a cold shiver through me. And even though Dr. Grey was frightening, I hung onto his every word. In the context of the course material, he could express to us the terrifying nature of the vampire without dilution, in his sonorous voice with its beautiful diction.

I was sorry when Dr. Grey called the end of class and bid us farewell until the following Tuesday. I headed out the door, congratulating myself on having gone safely unnoticed, when I heard him call out.

"Diana . . . that is your name, correct?"

I stopped, turned, and replied, "Yes."

He paused a moment, and I realized he was waiting for the last of my classmates to leave the room. He approached me and said, "I couldn't help noticing the ribbon."

I looked down at the cuff of my shirt and, sure enough, the ribbon was peeking out.

Why did I forget to take off the ribbon? I asked myself. I groaned as I considered the possibility that a part of me wanted to attract the professor's attention.

But Dr. Grey, now standing close enough that I could feel a faint coolness in the air, gave me a smile. "Can you stay a bit?" he asked me. He seemed, at that moment, the most harmless person imaginable.

So I stayed and talked to him.

Every week.

I can't say he concealed what he was from me, not at all. He even described to me what it was like to drink a mortal to death. It's appalling to tell you that I listened, trembling, but unwilling to leave, as he described the terrible ecstasy of drinking and drinking until the victim was pale and still, an empty shell in his embrace.

If only I had heeded my own sense of danger. If only I had quit that class. But I didn't, and that was the worst mistake I ever made concerning vampires, as you will soon see. . . .

chapter 9

When You Start Thinking of Coverting

onverting to vampirism is not a trivial matter. It's even beyond your everyday *serious* matters, like converting a Lutheran to a Catholic. If you change from Lutheran to Catholic, you're a mortal human being either way. If you become a vampire, your very nature is changed.

Clearly this is not a decision to be made without one of those Pro and Con Lists. So if you are at the point of giving it solemn consideration (and almost everyone arrives there, sooner or later), then it's time to get out your notepad and pen. I'm serious, really — I want you to write "PRO" and "CON" on the paper as you begin to weigh these issues carefully.

IMMORTALITY HAS ITS PERKS

Okay, start writing down your pros. Obviously there is no shortage of pros to being a vampire. Wouldn't it be grand not to have to pay life insurance premiums, get flu shots, or sit out the possible dancing-in-the-flames at the end of your mortal life? Meanwhile, it certainly would not suck to have qualities like vampires have. Imagine the awesomeness if you could conjure up faeries, build yourself a fabulous lair, and stun everyone with your sex appeal.

If you picture your vampire self, in all her glory, you will see what I mean. No doubt she is prettier than Princess Grace of Monaco, can actually *throw* a baseball and not just trickle it ten feet, and writes so beautifully that every book she authors hits the *New York Times* Bestseller List. No, wait — that would be *my* vampire self. But you catch my drift.

Supreme among all your reasons is this: you are head-over-heels in love with some vampire, and you want that union formalized, set in stone for eternity, consummated on a supernatural plane, etc. That's what makes you want to be a vampire . . . you want to be *his* vampire.

THE BIGGEST CON MAY SURPRISE YOU

Now that we have that fact out in the open, let's turn to the Con List . . . even though right now it seems like the sum of all Cons will pale compared to that one single Pro you wrote in such large letters. Nevertheless, there are negatives to becoming a vampire.

Things like:

- A certain alienation from all the mortals they've ever known and loved
- Watching non-vampire friends and relatives grow old and die
- The mirror problem
- No chance to go to your final rest

But you know what's always at the top of any vampire's Con List?

Here it is, and I kid you not: "Not being able to be anything but a vampire."

I bet you hadn't thought of that, but it's true. When you become a vampire, that's the sum and total of who you are. You will always be a blood-drinking creature of the night. Mortals, on the other hand, have almost unlimited potential. Mortals can become, well, vampires for one thing. But also zombies (I didn't say you would, just that you can), hosts for alien intelligences (not always a bad thing), angelic spirits, and so on.

In a less literal sense, mortals can play at being all kinds of things, like magicians, defiers of gravity, aliens, gods, oversize faeries, dwarves and hobbits; the list is endless. Vampires, again, are always vampires. Have you ever heard of a vampire pretending to be an elf or a space alien?

I know I referred at the beginning of the book to a vampire playing the lead in *Phantom of the Opera* on Broadway for one night. That worked because, in point of fact, the Phantom is pretty much a vampire, just without the bloodsucking. I know, right? And that's the biggest stretch you'll see a vampire make. He won't dress as a pirate for Halloween. And he won't ever be a zombie or a pod person or even an angelic spirit. Blood-drinking creature of the night — that's his entire repertoire.

And this, my friend, is the big Con to being a vampire — one you certainly need to ponder before you take the conversion plunge. No matter how sublime your vampire boyfriend, no matter how you adore him, no matter how awesomely excellent you would be in vampire form, it gives a person pause to consider the many, many doors that slam shut the moment you bite the neck of one undead.

WHEN THE BITE IS A GO

Be that as it may . . . let's assume for the time being that you've made up your mind to go immortal. How does conversion take place?

The recipe for making a vampire is simply this: vampire blood.

Typically, the converting vampire will give himself a good bite on the wrist, press the wound to the mortal's lips, and let her instantaneous wild hunger take over. She feeds, and the blood spreads through her system, converting her blood to the immortal stuff. That enchanted blood in turn converts her entire body to undeadness.

Sounds almost too easy, doesn't it? You might fear if you kiss a vampire's paper cut before it instantly heals, that could be enough to convert you! But, actually, a little bit of vampire blood won't turn you. There's a threshold you have to cross in terms of consumption level before there's enough blood in your system to accomplish the change.

Unfortunately, no one can be sure where that threshold is. And once you start drinking his blood, trust me, you will be disinclined to stop. It is Colin who describes the feeling best, I think. He says, "Imagine someone with whom you are wildly in love. Picture everything about him that makes your mind spin and your heart sing. Then imagine that stuff distilled down into a warm, steaming cup of something like hot chocolate only tasting just the way he makes you feel."

Yeah, and then imagine pushing away from it after one sip. As the saying goes, "Not bloody likely."

AFTER THE DEED IS DONE

All right then, you've done it. Blood quaffed, belly full, no turning back. What can you expect will happen?

Certainly if you were fighting off a cold before the bite, you have now won that war hands down. And there will be no more need to ask for help opening the pickle jar. Those transformations happen instantly. So do the other physical changes. Look in the mirror, I mean webcam, and you'll see you are paler than Gwyneth Paltrow in February, and can unfurl your fangs at will. (You will not, of course, see any lame albino cat contacts effect.) You will also be youthful enough, pretty enough, and shapely enough to shop in any department of any store at the mall that you choose.

I make light of the experience, but really, it is not so much a laughing matter. Several of my vampire friends have described their conversions in detail to me. And regardless of how they feel about immortal vs. mortal life, one and all agreed that it was an indescribably amazing experience. They found aches and pains gone that they didn't even realize they had. They didn't need to see a reflection to know how beautiful they had become: they could simply *feel* it. And the overwhelming sense of superiority was intoxicating, making it nearly impossible not to be high on your own hubris.

Hopefully you will have an opportunity to plan in advance for this death-changing event. If so, you'll take time to figure out the best timing and approach to informing friends and relatives. The advice I shared in Chapter 7 will help, but I can't pretend that it isn't going to be a challenge.

You'll need to have plenty of Liquid Shade handy, and I'd advise you to avoid sunlight till you've been dosing yourself for a week. (So don't convert when a pressing deadline may happen at work or when you have a trip to Vegas scheduled.) Also, stock up on synthblood — no vampire is ever without a supply of that. The vampire that converted you will stick to you like glue for awhile, just to make sure you get the hang of everything. They're good about that — everyone remembers what it was like to be a new convert.

All this sounds hunky-dory, doesn't it? No weirder than Orientation Week at college, really, and without the stress of locating all your classes. But it will not be exactly hunky-dory. Not good, not bad, just very, very, very strange. Just ask any vampire about his first month as an immortal.

WHEN IT'S SOMEONE ELSE'S IDEA

If at this point you are not so sure converting is for you after all, another question may have arisen in your mind. In the movies, you most often see people converted against their will. What if you don't want to be undead, but some vampire has decided for you?

As you can probably guess based on everything else I've told you, there are very few vampires who are nasty enough to do such a thing. Nevertheless, in life there are exceptions to every rule. Once in a red moon you'll meet a vampire determined, out of cruelty or out of obsessive desire, to make you one of his kind.

Don't let your fascination with such a fellow get in the way of prudence. You can be so enamored that you ignore the bad vibes, and fail to heed your instincts for self-preservation. I'm talking about more than an evil vampire's ability to enchant you into submission; sometimes it's your own will, your own desires, that blind you to the danger. Then, suddenly, there's vampire blood on your tongue and it's too late.

Too late.

But is there no way to fight back? Well, garlic may slow a vampire down, but it won't stop him. Nor will crucifixes or holy water. And if you're thinking you can successfully kill him, all I can say is, I'm an expert on the undead, and even I would not have such an aspiration. I would certainly not be irresponsible enough to try to teach you how.

When it comes to messing with vampires who want to convert you against your will, an ounce of prevention is worth a ton of cure. Especially considering that a cure is very, very unlikely.

Case Study 109:

Me, Conner, and Sven, and how I made the choice.

I won't try to deny it: I'm useless in the face of my affection for Conner and I'm certain I always will be. And as no doubt you guessed by now, he is the one vampire I was willing to convert for.

Unfortunately, he was also the one vampire I knew who seemed to truly envy mortals. As I got to know him more intimately, I began to be convinced of this. He could at times be quite melancholy about it.

One evening, as we sat on the roof of my house watching the sunset (yes, vampires do love to sit in unconventional and high places), Conner was in such a mood. I wanted desperately to lift his spirits, and I got it into my head that there was one way to achieve that goal: telling him I wanted to convert for him.

He turned to me and his eyes met mine, with a look so forbidding it brought tears to my eyes. "You may convert if you wish," he said evenly, "but not by *my* blood."

I had never seen him so fiercely angry, not even during our spat about Dr. Grey, and it frightened me. It also frustrated me terribly, because it was the "by his blood" I was truly interested in, not the conversion. I wanted to discuss the matter, but he clearly did not . . . so that was the end of that discussion.

Or should have been. But I, of course, didn't want to let it go. I thought about finding another vampire, asking him to turn me, and then presenting myself to Conner with the deed a *fait accompli*. Perhaps Conner actually wished I were a vampire; he simply wanted me to make a free choice. Or something like that, I told myself.

About this time something rather ironic happened: I met a vampire who was tall and blond, with broad shoulders and one of those scruffy short beards we women go so gaga for. Yes, just like Conner had once joked to me. Sven didn't sing like an angel, didn't have a private plane, and didn't make up poetry. No, it was worse than that: Sven was a dancer. Ballet, contemporary, Latin, ballroom, hip hop . . . the whole spectrum. And whatever style of dancing he picked on a particular day, he did it *sexy*. As in making-you-want-to-eat-your-own-soul kind of sexy.

Sven was not as grounded and cerebral as Conner . . . Sven liked mortal women, dancing, and taking mortal women dancing, and if he could have those things he was as happy as a pig in mud. He didn't come anywhere close to touching my soul the way Conner did, but I certainly loved to go dancing with him. And in those days, Conner made me feel all pine-y and anguished, so dancing with Sven was a cheerful relief.

One night Sven took me home and we sat on my front porch talking for awhile, even though conversation was not a typical activity for us. In his sweet tenor, with his Swedish accent, Sven asked if something was troubling me.

"In a nutshell, Sven," I said, "I'm in love with a vampire who is unwilling to convert me."

Sven cocked his blond head at me. "You wish to convert? In a nutshell, I can convert you. So what is the problem?'

I thought about trying to explain about Conner's blood and my feelings for it, but I suspected that would be hard to get across to him. Sven is the sort of vampire who never plays Gothic and is in a merry mood every day; how could he comprehend my angst? "Thanks for the offer, Sven," I said, "but . . ."

"You are in love with Conner, eh?" he asked me, trying to conceal a smile.

"Yes," I admitted.

"Then I can explain for you," said Sven. "I know about Conner.

Has he told you, when he was young and mortal he dreamt of being a vampire?"

"No," I admitted. "He hasn't told me much about that time of his life."

"Well, he did. And also he dreamt of being a prince, and a gypsy fortune teller, and I believe also a warlock-conjuror. I think to this day he wishes to be those things, and others as well, but he cannot be. For he is just a vampire. And so, he tells stories about all those other creatures, and must be content with the storytelling. Some days, though, he clearly is not." Sven paused, his face more serious than I had ever seen it. Then he said, "We immortals all have our regrets."

"Oh," I said, my eyes brimming with tears.

"If you still wish to convert, I can do it."

I blinked and looked into his face. "No, I think not, thank you, Sven," I told him.

He smiled and said, "You are welcome." And then he winked at me.

Sven was a bit deeper than I had given him credit for.

FAQS ABOUT THE UNDEAD

Q: Come on, isn't it true all you need to do to kill a vampire is put a stake through his heart?

A: Don't try to get me to address the issue, friend. I wish I could help you, but I know vampire society too well to even go there. Sorry!

Q: Is there any issue with blood type compatibility if you want to convert? I'm type A-positive and my vampire boyfriend is B-negative.

A: As you might expect, your vampire boyfriend's B-negative blood is no longer your run-of-the-mill B-neg. Prepare to change your donor card, my dear, because that A-pos won't even be able to put up a fight.

Q: If vampires can be movie actors, how can you say they can't pretend to be other things, like pirates and zombies?

A: Easy answer: They only accept vampire parts. If they played anything else, they would cease to be vampires, after all. You don't follow me? Well, think about it: Have you ever had a crush on an actor because he played a vampire in a movie . . . and then you saw him in another role or in real life . . . and he simply wasn't the guy you fell in love with? Of course you have. So there, that proves my point: when an actor-vampire plays some other role, he ceases to be a vampire. Works exactly the same way for a vampire-actor. Still confused? Well, just take my word for it, this is a very important concept and remembering it will serve you well in a surprising number of ways.

chapter 10

My Personal Recommendations for the Perfect Vampire Relationship

Well, at this point you are one well-informed ribbon-wearer, and privy to a treasure trove of helpful knowledge about vampire dating. You understand about the variety and splendor of this race of beings, and you've observed some different approaches to interacting with them.

Now it's time to determine what you, personally, want to do with what you know.

A TROUPE OF IMMORTALS OR VAMPIRE MONOGAMY: YOU CHOOSE

You see, each one of us will find our own unique ways of interacting with vampires. To a certain extent, your heart will lead you in this regard. If what you need is the fun, inspiration and encouragement of several different immortals simultaneously, you'll choose the route of courting and befriending more than one at a time. If your psyche needs strength and stability, or you're wrestling with a particular challenge, you may find the companionship of one special vampire to be more fulfilling.

So if you simply "go with the bloodflow," I predict you will find yourself drawn to precisely the right immortal(s), who will entertain, assist, and nurture you at any given point in time. It's funny how this works: vampire relationships often unfold and evolve quite apart from your intentions. For example, don't freak out if you find that a vampire who once fascinated you suddenly seems less captivating, and you want to turn to another instead.

Perhaps that seems like two-timing, and you may fear hurting your vampire with such behavior. Fortunately, I've found the undead quite understanding about such things. This is probably the result of their having so much time on their hands — they just don't sweat the small stuff. You know how we often say "Life's too short"? They often say, "Life's too long."

On the other hand, if one particular blood-drinker really captivates your fancy, there's nothing wrong with focusing your attention upon him alone for a good long while. In that case, it can be helpful to reflect upon what qualities of this particular vampire touch you so deeply. Often you can learn some valuable things about yourself from such musings, and that knowledge may help you in your regular life as well.

LET A VAMPIRE BE YOUR MENTOR

The undead make great mentors, and here's an example. I was never really the athletic sort in my younger days. However, as I got older I began to realize I needed to start exercising for my health's sake. It so happened that my closest vampire friend at the time, the aforementioned Gunnar, was an exercise nut. I know, weird, hey? If you're immortal, why would you bother? But Gunnar was into weight lifting and biking and such, and I really wanted to emulate him (as often happens when you're excited about a new vampire). It was my desire to be like Gunnar that helped me turn myself into a more athletic person.

I've used the same principle countless times in order to improve myself or get through challenges. Whether it be gathering courage for a public appearance, enduring the pain of surgery, standing up to oppressors, or surviving whatever life threw at me, I relied upon my vampire associates to augment my strength.

You see, you don't actually have to become a vampire to benefit from their superior powers and skills. Just knowing that there is an immortal in your corner can do you a world of good and your human relationships will benefit too. You can say to yourself, "What wisdom of Colin's would apply here?" or "How would Mordred deal with this cretin?" (Although in the latter case, you'd need to amend the question to " . . . short of disembowelment.") Interacting with your vampire friends truly does cause their powers to rub off on you a bit.

BALANCE IS KEY

You will probably also go through periods of wanting to hang with vampires all the time, and periods where other things take precedence and you forget all about them for awhile. This is perfectly natural, and again, vampires don't mind it. They remember what it's like to be mortal and only have a limited amount of time to get everything done. They respect our tendency to get distracted by other interests and responsibilities.

(A little aside here: Never feel that vampires depend upon you to exist, like Tinkerbell required belief in fairies to keep her alive. Vampires were here before you showed up, and will still be here after you're gone.)

My point here is that relationships with vampires cannot be forced. You can't force them to happen, nor can you force them *not* to happen. It's best simply to live and let live — or, rather, to live and let be undead — and just enjoy what unfolds.

A common mistake mortals make is to be so enchanted with vampires that we want that feeling of enchantment constantly. I have tried occasionally to demand my undead friends thrill and amuse me whenever I want. This approach fails to consider that key fact we covered in the beginning of this book: you can't tame a vampire. Sometimes no matter how much you wish your vampire boyfriend would transport you to fabulous realms beyond the beyond, it's not going to happen simply because you want it to. He may just want to surprise you one day, and it's hard to surprise someone who is constantly up in your face. Ease up, let him do his thing, and all will come right soon enough.

I have another theory for why vampire boyfriends sometimes absent themselves unexpectedly. I think they are very sensitive to the needs of the psyche, and are able somehow to perceive what needs to be done to keep their mortal girlfriends in balance. You should try to be as sensitive to your inner needs as he is. For example, if you spend a lot of time and energy on one immortal, eventually your psyche will start to compel you to meet a new vampire; maybe for no other reason than needing the thrill of someone new in your life. Or, if you've been intensely caught up with the undead for a period of time, you'll feel like doing something non-vampiric for awhile. As long as you're not thinking of hanging out with zombies, it's probably healthy to follow where your inner motivation leads. Pirates, perhaps?

Oh, and if you're worried about vampire jealousy, it's quite rare. Immortals are pretty fair-minded, and recognize that if they're not into monogamy, they shouldn't demand it of us either.

So in an ideal vampire relationship, balance is key . . . and that's something every immortal knows, even the mean and crazy ones (which is why the mean and crazy ones try to get you off balance). Love your vampire boyfriend . . . and your mortal one as well. Immerse yourself in one incredible Conner-like immortal . . . then spend some time with another, different sort of one, or two, or three. Celebrate the wonder of vampires . . . and remember that you are wonderful, too. Never lose your love of the undead . . . but invest time and energy as well into other areas of your life.

HERE'S THE BIG BONUS

Follow all my suggestions, and work out your own approach . . . and I am confident you too will be able to find a happy and fulfilling way to relate to vampires. Once you have, you'll discover a bonus reward in addition to the inherent benefits of vampire relationships. That is, you'll find yourself more able to give joy and love to the *mortal* in your life.

In my experience, there is just so much fun to be had with vampires that it simply makes one a happier person. It's similar to having regular vacations in which you travel to exotic places. Your travel experiences make you more interesting and well-rounded. Meanwhile, they break up regular workaday life with refreshing stimulation. For example, it's hard not to have a smile for the UPS man, when you spent the evening before learning to tango or flying over the Chrysler building. Having such a colorful life in the vampire world just makes you more interesting, more creative, and more fun. You may find that your vampire boyfriend encourages you to do all sorts of new things you didn't have the passion to attempt before, like ziplining or making felted animals. All this *joie de vivre* just spills over into the lives of those around you.

Some people think that hanging out with vampires makes people withdraw into their own little worlds, as if we retreat into coffins or dark caves lined with dangling bats. Nothing could be further from the truth. Vampire lovers expand rather than contract. They learn more about themselves and about all humankind. They find new ways to be brave, patient, loyal, kind, and creative. Ironically, befriending the undead simply makes a person more fully alive.

And sometimes, befriending the undead can literally *keep* you alive. . . .

Part Five:
Dr. Steven Grey/The Final Reckoning

I don't know why I kept going back, why I kept staying after class to talk to Dr. Grey. Maybe the fact that he kept a respectable distance lulled me into a false sense of safety. Maybe enjoying his supreme beauty and the palpable, delicious power of his presence made it worth the risks.

At any rate, every week we talked a little longer, and the last night of class we stayed nearly two hours. I was shocked at how long we'd sat there, him on the edge of the big desk, me in my seat looking up at him like a disciple. I told him, regretfully, that I really had to get home.

He walked me to my car, and we said goodnight . . . in fact, we said goodbye.

My car wouldn't start. The battery was dead. I was sitting there, staring at the dashboard trying to decide whom to call, when there was a tap on the driver's side window. I rolled it down.

"Car trouble?" asked Dr. Grey.

"My battery, I think. Do you by chance have jumper cables?"

He frowned. "I'm afraid not. Could I give you a ride somewhere?"

"If you could just give me a ride home — I can have someone jump it in the morning."

In the back of my mind a little voice said, "*What the hell are you doing?*"

"Of course, Diana," said the professor, "it's the least I can do."

I locked up my car and followed him to his, a beautiful

midnight blue Corvette. My mind whirred, but the prevailing thought was that if Dr. Grey truly wanted to hurt me, he could have done so long ago. Hadn't he proven his benevolence toward me by now? Weren't we friends, as unlikely as that had once seemed? I got in his car and a few minutes later we arrived at my house. I turned to him, and in that moment he seemed kinder, friendlier, more harmless than ever.

"Would you like to come in for some coffee?" I asked him.

As we sat on my living room sofa, sipping our coffee and talking, it seemed surreal. I tried to tell myself this vampire was the very fellow Conner considered his nemesis, but I found it difficult to grasp that.

And then, as if he had read my mind — which vampires can't do — Dr. Grey said, "So, I've heard you are a good friend of Conner's."

My heart raced. "Yes . . . yes, I am," I told him, afraid to say a word more.

"I know he isn't my biggest fan, to say the least. But I have tremendous admiration for the man. He possesses one of the most creative minds I've ever known, and I've known some brilliant men."

"I know," I agreed, lamely. "His stories are amazing."

"I haven't had the pleasure of his company for quite awhile. You must give him my best." Then he laughed. "Although I'm sure he won't accept it. No doubt you know we don't see eye to eye."

Tongue-tied, I tried to think of what to say.

"Did he warn you about me?" asked Dr. Grey.

Vampires can't read minds but they are generally very good at faces, so there was no point in lying. "Yes," I said.

"He would, of course. But you see, there's nothing to fear. I can't understand why vampires can't disagree without it coming to hostilities. He and I are brothers, after all. And we have more shared history than I imagine he mentioned to you."

His apparent magnanimity shocked me. "You don't hate him?" I asked.

He laughed again, almost too good-naturedly. "Well, I'd say I don't, but I'm guessing you wouldn't believe me." He leaned closer to me, giving me a long, hard look. "Of more interest is the fact that you really care for him," he said, raising one brow and smiling. Then he added, "Enough to want to drink of him, I'd venture."

I hadn't thought vampires could read faces *that* well. "Um . . ." I began.

He broke in, "It's just that I know Conner quite well, and I know therefore what a hardship it would be to want to be close to the fellow. Close . . . forever. As I'm sure you have wished. I can see on your face how unhappy you are on this subject, Diana." He took my hand in his cool one — the first time he had actually touched me. He continued, "I know Conner. Perhaps more accurately than he knows himself."

"What do you mean?" I asked.

Dr. Grey fixed me with his gaze, all the while stroking my hand in his. "I know he is very, very lonely. There's really only one thing he's wanted, ever since he was converted — an eternal companion. But here's his curse: his moral compunctions tell him such a thing would be a hideous crime. He couldn't bear the guilt of it. So you see the poor soul's predicament. He cannot bring himself to take the only thing he wants. I've long believed his only hope is to find someone who would have another do the deed in his stead, and then present herself to him, already turned. But in all these centuries, no woman like that has appeared. At least not until now . . ."

His eyes, those ominously gleaming eyes, were on me once more.

I'm not sure why it was that exact moment when I finally woke up from my long delusion about Dr. Steven Grey. Perhaps he had come too close to saying exactly what I'd always wanted to hear, and thus I saw that the whole experience with him had been too good to be anything but really bad.

At any rate, I was thinking clearly now, and I was terrified. So far Dr. Grey was using only persuasion to have his way with me, but if he decided to mesmerize me, I would be helpless. I knew I had better get him out of my house before he recognized my new state of mind. I thought fast.

"Dr. Grey, you really make me think," I said. "I wonder . . . but I can't make up my mind about such a thing tonight. I have to sleep on it. But I trust that if I do decide — then you would help."

He smiled at me. The smile broadened, until his perfect teeth began to show, with barely extended incisors. Then he said, "You're on to me."

I tried not to gasp.

He continued, "I came so close. Now you've really spoiled it for me. I so wanted to persuade you to voluntarily choose the very thing that would make that fool Conner eternally unhappy with the both of you. But no matter."

My eyes were fully open then: I saw with perfect clarity the stupid self-destructiveness of my choices to that point. But, of course, it was too late. One minute I was full of contrition and regret, desperately determined to repel Dr. Grey . . . and the next he had me utterly in his power. Whatever he wanted me to feel, I was going to feel nothing but that, a raging hunger for his blood. And when he drew one amazingly sharp fingernail across the side of his throat and I saw the crimson stripe well up, I flung myself upon his cold, velvet neck and drank.

The blood drinking was not exactly as I had imagined it, or as I had pictured it with Conner, with the taste of Conner upon my tongue, and the warmth of Conner filling my belly and spreading into my limbs. No, it was Dr. Grey, but he was no less glorious to feed upon than any rapturously perfect vampire would be, evil or no.

After I had taken a taste, he withdrew his mesmerization power and left me to my desperate hunger. I was not about to stop myself, not for all the gold In El Dorado. So I drank, and my will and self-awareness blurred and melted, and I didn't care, until I had sunk into utter delirious oblivion.

Oblivion except for the tiny whisper in my head that was screaming in abject terror.

Some time passed.

I was floating, in a formless mist of a most soothing gray color, and I heard a voice, a distant voice, crying out, far away. It got closer, and louder, till I heard it say, "Oh no, no, no — not this, no, no, no!"

I recognized the voice . . . it was Conner's.

Arms lifted me. It got darker, and then I was lying down somewhere cramped. Then I was moving. I got lost awhile, then found myself lying somewhere not so cramped, and softer.

He was calling my name, and I had the sense he had been doing so for some time. I heard a question, a question I felt he had repeated many times. "When did you drink from him, Diana? What time was it? I need to know!"

It seemed an impossible question at first, but it was Conner asking, and with such urgency and panic in his normally composed voice. I calculated. Class ended at. . . . We talked till. . . . Drove. Talked. "Ten-thirty," I said, hoping that was the right answer.

"Thank God," he said.

I opened my eyes and found I could see him now. Very vividly. "Am I a vampire now, Conner?" I asked, weakly.

He looked like he was crying. It shocked me to see such grief on his face. "Did you do this to be with me?" he asked, his voice catching.

"I didn't want to. He made me."

At my words Conner's face brightened a little, and then determination came into his eyes. "You are not a vampire if I can help it," he said.

Conner put me to sleep then, and much to my amazement, being put to sleep by Conner was even more wonderful than anything I had felt previously that night.

And this is how I came to learn the Vampire Escape Clause.

When you drink a vampire's blood, it starts converting your mortal blood into its same immortal form. And once all your blood has converted, it starts working on the rest of you. Once it gets to working on the rest of you, it's too late. But if you are caught early, and a very clever vampire is at hand with a large supply of synthblood and the right equipment, the process can be reversed.

Earlier Conner had felt a strange unease on my behalf, and had decided to check on me. He was just driving up my street as Dr. Grey departed my driveway in his Corvette. Filled with terrible dread and fearing the worst, Conner burst in my front door and found me catatonic on the sofa.

He drove me to his house at some ridiculous rate of speed, wondering all the while if he was too late. He hoped to drain all my tainted blood from me before it turned me completely . . . but if too much time had passed, Conner would accomplish nothing and I would become "bloodless vampire" — a frightful vampire/zombie hybrid. On the other hand, if he had caught the process early enough, he might yet be able to save me.

"Ten-thirty" gave him hope, so he decided to risk it. He had an emergency kit (everything you need for a complete and total exsanguination) and enough synthblood to replace every pint in my body. That would keep me alive until he could round up a supply of my type of human blood (vampires actually have clearinghouses for that sort of thing) and repeat the transfusion, restoring me to total mortal normalcy.

All this I learned a few hours later, when I woke up after the first transfusion. I was tucked into Conner's bed, and he was lying next to me, fully clothed, on top of the bedclothes. The way I found him staring at me, I wondered if he had been watching for hours.

"Thank god you're all right!" he exclaimed when I opened my eyes.

"Oh, Conner, what happened?" I asked him.

He told me. When he was finished, he said, "I've never done that before and I swear I don't ever want to have to do it again. Vampire life is not supposed to involve sudden life-or-undeath rescues of damsels in distress, and race-against-the-clock suspense, and trying to find where the hell you put the alcohol wipes."

Conner indeed looked wrung out. Ashamed of what I'd put him through, I said, "I should have listened to you. I'm sorry, Conner."

"You should have. And I accept your apology. Now promise me you are wiser."

"I promise. Dr. Grey . . . he made me bite him. I wouldn't have done it of my own free will. You believe me, don't you?"

Conner gave me a solemn nod. "I do."

"I love you, Conner, but I have to love you as a mortal. It's just my calling to be a mortal."

He smiled, in a way that was, in the larger part, happy. "I know. Nevertheless you must swear to love me forever."

"I swear to love you forever," I told him.

"And I you," he said.

"Thank you," I said, and reached for his cold hand, and brought it to my lips, and kissed it.

He smiled, and this time it was completely happy.

HAPPILY EVER AFTER

So that, my friends, is how that particular story ended, and happily I remain a mortal.

Emphasis on the word "happily."

Many people make the mistake of believing there is inherent tragedy in falling for one of the undead. There he is, immortal, never changing, an alien in our world. And here you are, a mortal, imperfect, at the mercy of time. How can such a relationship work out happily, really? Is it not a macabre Romeo-and-Juliet tale, doomed to tragedy?

In fact, that viewpoint is, as my life attests, quite untrue. It is based upon faulty reasoning. You see, there are some things in life that are eternal and beyond the grasp of our understanding. There are some things that are ideal and sublime, and by their nature inspire our adoration. If this were not true, no one would ever fall in love at all, and it happens every day.

And when you fall really hard, the way a ribbon-wearer feels about vampires, it's for life . . . and beyond. I wasn't indulging in romantic hyperbole when I told Conner I would love him forever. He wasn't conveniently disregarding my mortality when he replied in kind. I didn't need to turn away from mortal life to be with him — I'm with him every time I am inclined to be. And that, I suspect, will be the case just as long as he lives.

And you know how long that is.

GO FORTH AND LOVE VAMPIRES

Well, my dear vampirophilic friends, this concludes my little guide-book! You have the knowledge, you have the tools, and of course you have the motivation. Yes, you're as ready as you'll ever be.

So tie on that red satin ribbon . . .

catch yourself a vampire . . .

and love him forever.